Congressional Research Service

Child Welfare: Structure and Funding of the Adoption Incentives Program along with Reauthorization Issues

Emilie Stoltzfus
Specialist in Social Policy

April 18, 2013

Congressional Research Service

7-5700

www.crs.gov

R43025

CRS Report for Congress ——————————————————————

Prepared for Members and Committees of Congress

Summary

Under the Adoption Incentives program (Section 473A of the Social Security Act) states earn federal bonuses when they increase adoptions of children who are in need of new permanent families. All 50 states, the District of Columbia, and Puerto Rico have earned a part of the $375 million in Adoption Incentive funds that have been awarded since the program was established as part of the Adoption and Safe Families Act of 1997 (ASFA, P.L. 105-89). Funding authorized for this program has been extended twice since it was established, most recently in 2008 (P.L. 110-351), but is currently set to expire on September 30, 2013. Congress may act to revise and/or extend this program in the 113th Congress.

Congress has long shown interest in improving the chances of adoption for children who cannot return to their parents and who might otherwise spend their childhoods in temporary foster homes before "aging out" of foster care. Since ASFA's enactment in 1997, the annual number of children leaving foster care for adoption has risen from roughly 30,000 to more than 50,000 and the average length of time it took states to complete the adoption of a child from foster care declined by close to one year (from about four years to less than three). Over the same time period, and in significant measure due to the greater number of children leaving foster care for adoption and at a faster pace, the overall number of children who remain in foster care declined by 29%—from a peak of 567,000 in FY1999 to 401,000 in FY2011. Despite these successes, however, the number of children "waiting for adoption" (104,000 on the last day of FY2011) remains more than double the number of children who are adopted during a given year. Adoptions of older children remain far less common than adoptions of younger children, and some 26,000 youth aged out of foster care in FY2011, compared to just 19,000 in FY1999.

Under the current Adoption Incentive bonus structure, states earn $4,000 for each adoption of a foster child that is above the number of foster child adoptions finalized by the state in FY2007 and $8,000 for each adoption of an older child (9 years or older) above the number of older child adoptions it finalized in FY2007. If a state has earned an award in either of those categories—or if it improves its adoption rate—it earns $4,000 for each adoption of a special needs child (under age 9) that is above the number of such adoptions it finalized in FY2007. For improving its rate of adoption (above the rate it achieved in FY2002 or a later year with a higher rate), a state is eligible for additional incentive funds of $1,000 multiplied by the increased number of adoptions that are calculated to have resulted from the improved adoption rate. However, increases in incentive amounts states earn due to improved adoption rates are only paid to those states if sufficient program appropriations are available after all awards for increases in the number of adoptions have been made.

In the four years (FY2008-FY2011) that the *current* incentive structure has been in place, states were eligible for incentive payments of $166 million. Of that amount, states earned $74 million for increases in the number of foster child adoptions, $45 million for increases in older child adoptions, and $37 million for increases in special needs (under age 9) adoptions, and they were eligible for increases of $10 million in their incentive payments for improvements in their rates of adoption. However, most appropriations provided for the Adoption Incentives program were needed to pay awards for the increased number of adoptions, and states received less than $2 million of the incentives for which they were eligible due to improved rates. Therefore, states are expected to receive no more than $158 million of the $166 million of the bonus funds for which they were eligible for adoptions finalized in FY2008-FY2011.

States are permitted to use Adoption Incentive bonuses to support a broad range of child welfare services to children and families. Many states report spending incentive funds on adoption-related child welfare purposes, including post-adoption support services, recruitment of adoptive homes, and training or conferences to improve adoption casework. A smaller number of states report using these funds for adoption assistance payments, improved adoption homes studies, child protection casework, foster care maintenance payments, or other child welfare purposes.

Funding for the Adoption Incentives program is provided on a discretionary basis as part of the annual appropriations process. The program is authorized to receive $43 million annually (through FY2013), but in recent years actual appropriations have been around $39 million. Final FY2013 appropriations for the Adoption Incentives program were included in the Consolidated and Further Continuing Appropriations Act, 2013 (P.L. 113-6) at this same level. However, those appropriations are subject to a 5% reduction (under the March 1 sequestration order).

At a February 27, 2013, hearing of the House Ways and Means Subcommittee on Human Resources, witnesses called for reauthorization of the Adoption Incentives program and especially stressed the need to find and support permanent families for older youth and other harder to place youth.

As part of its FY2014 budget request, the Administration calls for reauthorization of the program and proposes requiring states to spend their Adoption Incentive funds on "trauma-informed services to improve social and emotional well-being of children waiting for adoption or those having achieved adoption." The Administration does not propose other changes to the program and it seeks FY2014 funding for Adoption Incentives at the same level that was provided in FY2012 ($39 million).

Contents

Introduction.. 1
 Congressional Interest in Adoptions from Foster Care.. 1
 Adoptions with Public Child Welfare Agency Involvement... 2
  Growth in the Number of Adoptions Out of Foster Care 3
  Decline in Children in Foster Care Waiting for Adoption... 3
  Reduced Time to Adoption... 4
Adoption Incentives.. 4
 How Do States Earn Incentive Funds?.. 5
 Amount of Incentives 5
 Eligibility for Adoption Incentive Awards.. 6
 Awards and Appropriations 6
 Awards by Category for Adoptions Finalized in FY2008-FY2011 9
  Foster Child Adoptions.. 10
  Older Child Adoptions 10
  Special Needs (Under Age 9) Adoptions.. 11
  Adoption Rate 11
 Spending Award Money 12
Selected Reauthorization Issues... 13
 Continued Need For and Focus of Incentives 13
 Permanence for Older Children... 13
 Baseline Adjustment.. 14
 Availability of Awards for Improved Rate of Adoption.. 14
 Use of Incentive Funds 15
Related Legislative Actions in the 113th Congress.. 16

Tables

Table 1. Adoption Incentives: Summary of Appropriations and Award History............................ 8

Table 2. Adoption Incentives for Adoptions Completed in FY2008–FY2011 10

Table B-1. Adoptions with Public Child Welfare Agency Involvement, FY1995-FY2011 20

Table B-2. Number of Children Waiting for Adoption and Percentage of Waiting Children
 Adopted, FY1998-FY2011 21

Table B-3. Average and Median Length of Time to Finalized Adoption, In Months,
 FY2000-FY2011 22

Table C-1. Evolution of Adoption Incentives Bonus Structure... 23

Table D-1. Foster Child Adoptions and Incentives Earned for FY2008-FY2011 25

Table D-2. Older Child (Age 9 or Above) Adoptions and Incentives Earned, FY2008-
 FY2011 27

Table D-3. Special Needs (Under Age 9) Adoptions and Incentives Earned, FY2008-
 FY2011 29

Table D-4. Adoption Rates and Incentive Increases for Improved Adoption Rate 31

Table D-5. Incentives Earned by Award Category for Adoptions Finalized in FY2008-FY2011 34

Table E-1. Children in Foster Care on the Last Day of the Fiscal Year by State, FY2007-FY2011 37

Table E-2. Children Waiting for Adoption, FY2007-FY2011, Percentage Change in the Number of Those Children and Share Adopted by State 39

Appendixes

Appendix A. Glossary of Terms 18

Appendix B. Trends in Adoptions with Public Child Welfare Agency Involvement 20

Appendix C. Adoption Incentive Bonus Structure 23

Appendix D. Adoptions and Incentives Earned by Category and State 25

Appendix E. Children in Foster Care and Waiting for Adoption by State 37

Contacts

Author Contact Information 41

Introduction

The Adoption Incentives program (Section 473A of the Social Security Act) provides federal bonus funds to state child welfare agencies that increase adoptions of children who are in need of new permanent families. Generally, these are children for whom reuniting with their biological parents is not possible and who would otherwise be expected to remain in public foster care until they "age out" (that is, reach the state age of majority or the age at which state custody of children in foster care is ended). The first awards under the program were made to states (in FY1999) for improvements in numbers of adoptions in FY1998 and the most recent were made (in FY2012) for improvements in numbers of adoptions in FY2011. Through FY2012, more than $375 million in bonus funds have been awarded under the Adoption Incentives program. Currently states are eligible to receive these incentives for increases in adoptions finalized through FY2012 and funding to pay those bonuses is authorized through FY2013.

The 113th Congress will likely consider whether to extend the Adoption Incentives program. This report discusses background related to this program, including the longstanding Congressional interest in domestic adoption and the significant increases in adoptions from foster care that have occurred since the middle 1990s. It discusses the current program, including the incentive structure. State child welfare agencies may receive separate bonuses for increases in the number of adoptions of (1) foster children, (2) older children (9 years or older), and (3) children under age 9 who are determined to have "special needs." In addition, they may be eligible for increases in their incentive awards for an improved rate of adoption. The report also includes a discussion of some issues Congress may consider as part of the reauthorization debate and it notes reauthorization-related activities.

Throughout this report some unique terms related to adoption, foster child adoptions, or the Adoption Incentives program are used, e.g., "special needs" and "adoption rate." While each of these terms is explained in the body of the report, for ease of reference, they are also included in a "Glossary of Terms" provided in **Appendix A** to this report.

Congressional Interest in Adoptions from Foster Care

Foster care is a temporary living arrangement for children for whom remaining in their own homes is not safe or appropriate. Most children who enter foster care are ultimately reunited with their parents. However, when reunification is determined not possible or appropriate, adoption is generally considered the best way to achieve a new permanent family for a child.

Congress has long shown an interest in encouraging adoptions of children who would otherwise remain in foster care until they age out. In 1978, the Adoption Opportunities program (Title II of the Child Abuse Prevention and Treatment and Adoption Reform Act, P.L. 95-266) was enacted to require federal administrative coordination of adoption and foster care programs and to support research and other activities to "facilitate elimination of barriers to adoption and to provide permanent and loving home environments for children who would benefit from adoption, particularly children with special needs." In 1980, Congress enacted the Adoption Assistance and Child Welfare Act (P.L. 96-272), including the first federal support for ongoing subsidies to eligible adoptees with "special needs" (under a new Title IV-E of the Social Security Act). In this context the "special needs" designation applies to children in need of new permanent families (i.e., they cannot be returned to their parents) and who have conditions or factors that makes it harder to find them adoptive homes without offering assistance. States may establish their own factors to determine special needs, but commonly use factors such as a child's older age; membership in a sibling group; medical condition; mental, physical or emotional disability; or membership in a minority race/ethnicity.[1]

By 1997, a renewed concern about the failure to move children from foster care to permanent families was an important impetus for the Adoption and Safe Families Act (ASFA, P.L. 105-89). As part of that law, Congress made changes to federal child welfare policy that were intended to ensure that states focused on achieving expeditious permanence for children in foster care, including through adoptions whenever appropriate. Among other changes, the law tightened or added new permanency planning timelines for children in foster care, required states to spend certain federal child welfare funds (under the Promoting Safe and Stable Families Program) for adoption promotion and support services, and authorized financial bonuses to states that increase adoptions of children out of foster care under the newly created Adoption Incentives program.[2,3]

Adoptions with Public Child Welfare Agency Involvement

Adoption is a social and legal process by which a child gains a new and permanent family. For each child in foster care who cannot be reunited with his or her parents and for whom adoption is determined to be the child's route to permanency, the state must identify suitable and willing adoptive parent(s). States may begin the process of recruiting an adoptive family before a child is "legally free" for adoption. However, before the child's adoption may be finalized a state (or tribal) court must generally terminate any existing parental rights or responsibilities to a child. Once this process, referred to as "TPR" (for termination of parental rights), has been completed, the child's adoption by new parents may be finalized by a state or tribal court.[4]

Since the 1997 enactment of ASFA, the annual number of adoptions out of foster care rose significantly and the rate of adoptions has doubled. There are fewer children in foster care who are "waiting for adoption," and the average time it takes to complete an adoption has declined by roughly one year. At the same time, the number of children waiting for adoption remains more than double the number of those adopted each year and adoptions of older children remain less common than those of younger children.

---

[1] See "Conditions or Factors Used by States in Determining Special Needs," in CRS Report R42792, *Child Welfare: A Detailed Overview of Program Eligibility and Funding for Foster Care, Adoption Assistance and Kinship Guardianship Assistance under Title IV-E of the Social Security Act*, by Emilie Stoltzfus.

[2] CRS Report RL30759, *Child Welfare: Implementation of the Adoption and Safe Families Act (P.L. 105-89)*, by Karen Spar.

[3] In 2008, as part of the Fostering Connections to Success and Increasing Adoptions Act (P.L. 110-351) Congress expanded eligibility for Title IV-E adoption assistance by removing income criteria tied to the family from which a child had been removed (usually this is the child's biological family). The revised eligibility criteria are being phased in and now apply to only some children determined to have special needs. However, as of FY2018, any child determined by a state to have special needs may be eligible for ongoing, federally supported adoption assistance. See CRS Report RL34704, *Child Welfare: The Fostering Connections to Success and Increasing Adoptions Act of 2008 (P.L. 110-351)*, by Emilie Stoltzfus and "Federal Adoption Assistance Eligibility Criteria" in CRS Report R42792, *Child Welfare: A Detailed Overview of Program Eligibility and Funding for Foster Care, Adoption Assistance and Kinship Guardianship Assistance under Title IV-E of the Social Security Act*, by Emilie Stoltzfus.

[4] Adoptions are generally a matter of state law and most termination of parental rights (TPR) proceedings and adoption finalizations occur in state courts (although they may also occur in tribal courts). While TPR is required for nearly all adoptions, a few states (and certain tribes) recognize "tribal customary adoptions," which do not require TPR.

Growth in the Number of Adoptions Out of Foster Care

The annual number of adoptions from foster care climbed from less than 30,000 in the mid-1990s, to a peak of some 57,000 in FY2009. Since then (through FY2011) the number has remained at, or above, roughly 50,000. The rise in the number of adoptions played a significant role in the decline in the overall number of children in foster care, which peaked in FY1999 at 567,000 children and had declined by 29%, to 401,000 children, as of the last day of FY2011.[5]

The fact that the number of foster child adoptions has remained relatively high, despite the decline in the overall number of children in foster care, is notable. Viewed as a rate—that is the number of children adopted during a given fiscal year for every 100 children who were in foster care on the last day of the preceding fiscal year—public child welfare agency adoptions doubled since the late 1990s (from a rate of roughly 6 adoptions per 100 children in foster care to 12 per 100). (See **Table B-1** in **Appendix B** for annual data on number and rate of adoptions.)

Decline in Children in Foster Care Waiting for Adoption

For roughly one-quarter of the children in foster care on a given day, adoption has been identified as their case plan goal—that is, their exit strategy to permanency.[6] Some children with a permanency goal of adoption, and certain other children in foster care, are "legally free" for adoption—meaning the rights of both parents have been terminated. These children—those with a case plan goal of adoption and/or for whom all parental rights have been terminated are generally referred to as children who are "waiting for adoption."[7]

For most of FY1998-FY2011, the number of children waiting for adoption was between 130,000 and 135,000. However, in recent years this number has declined and it stood at 104,000 as of the last day of FY2011. Additionally, the share of waiting children who leave foster care for adoption generally grew across this time period. Specifically, the number of children adopted from foster care in FY1999 was 37% of all children waiting for adoption on the last day of FY1998; the comparable percentage for children adopted in FY2011 was 46%. (See **Table B-2** in **Appendix B** for annual data on the number of waiting children and the share adopted in the following year.)

Even though the number of waiting children has declined, that number represents a slightly larger share of the overall foster care caseload in FY2011 (26%) than was the case in FY1998 (22%). This relatively modest increase in share of children in foster care waiting for adoption—coinciding with greater success in moving waiting children to adoption—might reflect changes in state practice regarding who may be assigned a case goal of adoption. Alternatively, or in addition, it might be the

---

[5] From the late FY1990s through FY2005, the annual number of children entering foster care remained fairly stable even as the national foster care caseload declined. This was due to more, and faster, exits of children from foster care via adoption (and to some extent guardianship). From FY2006 through FY2011, the continued decline of the national caseload has been driven by both a decline in the number of children entering foster care each year, as well as a continuation of relatively high numbers of exits to adoptions.

[6] The most common case plan goal for children in foster care is to reunite with their parents. Smaller numbers of children in care have a case plan goal of living with another relative or living with a legal (relative or non-relative) guardian. Aside from these goals (and adoption), each of which plan for a child's exit from care to a permanent family, some youth in care have a goal of "emancipation" (leaving care as an "independent" adult) and others are assigned the goal of "long-term foster care." See HHS, ACF, ACYF, Children's Bureau, *The AFCARS Report, No. 19* (July 2012).

[7] For a more complete definition of "waiting children" see Glossary of Terms in **Appendix A**.

result of state efforts to reduce unnecessary entries to foster care—which in turn could mean a higher percentage of those entering will need to find a new permanent family via adoption.

Reduced Time to Adoption

Adoption is a multi-step legal and social process that takes time to accomplish. Children who enter foster care do not typically move directly to adoption. With limited exceptions federal policy requires that a state must make "reasonable efforts" to reunite a child with his or her family.[8] When reunification is determined not possible however, the state must take certain steps to free a child for adoption. Specifically, as amended by ASFA, federal law requires a state to petition a state court for termination of parental rights (TPR) to the child if a state court finds either that the child is an abandoned infant (as defined in state law) or that reasonable efforts to reunite the child and his/her parents are not required (because the parent has committed one of certain heinous crimes against the child or his/her sibling). Additionally, once a child has been in foster care for 15 out of the last 22 months, the state must petition the court for TPR, unless it can document for the court that doing so would not be in the child's best interest, that services necessary for reunification and agreed to in the child's case plan have not been provided, or that the child is living with a relative.[9] The state court must then determine—based on state laws defining when parental rights may be severed—whether to grant TPR.[10] At the same time, for any child who cannot be reunited and whose case plan goal is adoption, the state agency must work to find an appropriate and willing adoptive family. Once this step is complete, and a child is successfully placed with the family, a state court must again act, this time to finalize the adoption and, as part of this process, to formally provide the adoptive parents with all legal parental rights and responsibilities for the child.

Since FY2000, the amount of time a child spends in foster care before leaving via a finalized adoption has declined by roughly one year. Most of this reduction in time is a result of the shorter time frame needed to reach TPR. However, there has also been some decline in the amount of time it takes to finalize a child's adoption after TPR is completed. On average, adoptions of children out of foster care that were finalized in FY2000 took just under four years to complete (45.9 months). By contrast, children who reached a finalized adoption in FY2011 did so, on average, in just under three years (34.0 months). (For annual data on average and median time from removal to finalized adoption see **Table B-3** in **Appendix B.**)

Adoption Incentives

Promoting the use of adoptions to ensure children who would otherwise remain in foster care have a permanent family has been a driving purpose of the Adoption Incentives program since its creation. The program has also sought to provide special incentives to states for adoptions of children who are considered harder to place in adoptive homes, including children with special

---

[8] See "Prevent Entry or Reunite Children with Their Parents" in CRS Report R42794, *Child Welfare: State Plan Requirements under the Title IV-E Foster Care, Adoption Assistance, and Kinship Guardianship Assistance Program* , by Emilie Stoltzfus.

[9] Ibid. See "Ensure Timely Placement in a New Permanent Family When Appropriate."

[10] TPR must be determined for each parent individually. For more information see Child Welfare Information Gateway, State Statutes Series, *Grounds for Involuntary Termination of Parental Rights* (2010).

---

needs and older children.[11] Established by ASFA in 1997 (at Section 473A of the Social Security Act) the Adoption Incentives program has been amended and extended twice: first, by the Adoption Promotion Act of 2003 (P.L. 108-145), and, more recently, by the Fostering Connections to Success and Increasing Adoptions Act of 2008 (P.L. 110-351).

Each reauthorization of Adoption Incentives has made some changes to the incentive structure used to determine awards, including the categories for which awards may be earned, the "baselines" used to determine improvement, and/or the amount of the individual incentive awards. The current incentive structure is described below. (**Appendix C** includes a table that shows development of the incentive structure across program reauthorizations.)

How Do States Earn Incentive Funds?

States may earn Adoption Incentive funds in four ways. For an increase in the

- number of children adopted out of foster care overall;

- number of children adopted at age 9 or older;

- number of children adopted with special needs and who are under the age of 9; or

- rate at which children are adopted from foster care.

Whether a specific state has increased the *number* of adoptions is determined by comparing the number of adoptions that the state finalized during the fiscal year to the number of such adoptions it finalized in FY2007 (the "baseline" year). A state is determined to have increased its *rate* of adoption if the percentage of children adopted from foster care (as a share of the number of all children in foster care in the prior year) is greater than it was in FY2002, or in any succeeding fiscal year prior to the year for which the award is being determined.

Amount of Incentives

An eligible state earns $4,000 for each foster child adopted above its baseline number of foster child adoptions and $8,000 for each older child (age 9 or above) adoption above its older child adoption baseline.[12] If a state has earned an award in either of those categories—or if it improves its adoption rate—it also earns $4,000 for each adoption of a special needs child (under age 9) that is above its baseline number of such adoptions. Finally, for an improvement in its rate of adoption, a state is eligible for additional incentive funds of $1,000 multiplied by the increased number of adoptions achieved by the state that are attributed to its improved adoption rate.[13]

---

[11] The Adoption Incentive program seeks to influence state child welfare agency behavior. Congress has, separately provided a tax credit to individuals who adopt children, including children with special needs. This "incentive" to adopt is not a part of the discussion in this report. However, for more information see, CRS Report RL33633, *Tax Benefits for Families: Adoption*, by Christine Scott.

[12] These awards are separately calculated. One child's adoption (if child is age 9 or older) may be counted for purposes of determining awards in both categories. However, a state that increases its foster child adoptions does not necessarily increase its older child adoptions (or vice versa). To earn awards in both categories, the state must show increases in both categories.

[13] An award for an improved rate is calculated by multiplying the state's baseline adoption rate (i.e., highest rate achieved in FY2002 or any subsequent year preceding year for which award is being determined) by the number of children in the state's foster care caseload on the last day of the fiscal year preceding the year for which the award is (continued...)

However, increases due to improved adoption rates may only be paid if sufficient program funding is available after all awards for increases in the number of adoptions have been made.

Eligibility for Adoption Incentive Awards

Any state (includes the 50 states, District of Columbia, and Puerto Rico) operating a Title IV-E program may be eligible to earn Adoption Incentive funds provided awards are authorized for that year.[14] Current law authorizes awards for adoptions finalized in FY2008-FY2012—and authorizes funds for that purpose through FY2013.

Further, to be eligible for Adoption Incentives, the state must provide—via the Adoption and Foster Care Analysis Reporting System (AFCARS)—the necessary data to calculate the incentive amounts. The state must also assure that it provides health insurance coverage to any adoptive child for whom the state determined the child has special needs—including those eligible for ongoing Title IV-E adoption assistance and those with special needs who are not eligible for this assistance.[15] In addition, no state may receive an award for an increase in the number of special needs adoptions of children under the age of 9, unless that state has also shown an increase in that same year of the number of foster child or older child adoptions (compared to what the state achieved in FY2007), or an increase in the state's rate of adoption (compared to the rate achieved by the state in FY2002, or any subsequent year with a higher rate that is prior to the year the award is earned).

Awards and Appropriations

The first Adoption Incentive awards were paid in FY1999 for adoptions finalized in FY1998 and the most recent were paid in FY2012 for adoptions finalized in FY2011. During the life of the program, all 50 states, the District of Columbia and Puerto Rico have earned Adoption Incentive payments in one or more years and more than $375 million has been awarded to all states through FY2012. Discretionary funding is authorized for the program through FY2013 at the annual level of $43 million. Actual appropriation levels have varied and in recent years have been at roughly $39 million annually. Final FY2013 appropriations for the Adoption Incentives program were included in the Consolidated and Further Continuing Appropriations Act, 2013 (P.L. 113-6) at this same level. However, that appropriation is subject to a 5% reduction (under the March 1 sequestration order).

Appropriations made as part of a given fiscal year's appropriation cycle are used to provide bonuses for increases in adoptions finalized in the previous fiscal year. For example, Adoption Incentives funding provided as part of the FY2012 appropriations cycle was awarded to states in

---

(...continued)

being determined. This result is then subtracted from the number of foster child adoptions in the state in the year for which the award is being determined. The difference represents the number of adoptions that are attributed to the increased adoption rate and this number (rounded to nearest whole number) is multiplied by $1,000 to determine the award amount. For an example of this award calculation see HHS, ACF, Information Memorandum, "Adoption Incentive Payments," September 1, 2009 (ACYF-CB-IM-09-03), p. 6.

[14] Section 473A(b)(1) of the Social Security Act. Tribes may not participate in this program. See HHS, ACF, ACYF-CB-IM-09-03, p. 1.

[15] Section 473A(b)(3) and (4) of the Social Security Act.

August 2012 for adoptions finalized in FY2011. If not all of the funds available in the Adoption Incentive account are needed to make incentive awards, these funds may typically be carried over and used for bonus awards in a subsequent year.[16] Alternatively, if funding is not sufficient to make full bonus awards for increases in the *number of adoptions*, HHS pro-rates awards earned and, assuming appropriations are made for the subsequent year, will use some of the funds from that following year to pay the remainder of the incentives earned. However, bonus increases related to an improvement in the state's *rate of adoption* are only paid after all incentive awards for increase in the number of adoptions have been made and, then, only to the extent that funding is available when those awards are initially made. If insufficient funds are available at the time the initial incentive amounts are awarded, only part, or none, of these increases are paid.[17]

Table 1 summarizes the appropriations provided and awards made by fiscal year for which the funds were initially appropriated and the fiscal year for which the incentive funds were earned. For numerous years, not all of the funding shown as the award amount for a given year was actually paid to states at a single time or in a single fiscal year. However, with the exception of FY2011 (discussed below), the total award amount shown was eventually paid once additional funding was provided for the program. For adoptions finalized in FY2011, 87% ($31.8 million) of the total award amount shown in **Table 1** ($36.5 million) was available to be awarded in FY2012. However, the additional $4.7 million is expected to be awarded to states in FY2013 (using FY2013 appropriations and before awards for adoptions finalized in FY2012 are made).

---

[16] Since its establishment, Section 473A(h)(2) has provided that funds appropriated for the Adoption Incentives program may be used in any fiscal year through the last fiscal year for which funding for the program is authorized (initially this was FY2003, then FY2008, and currently it is FY2013). However, the use of funds across years has usually been limited to fewer years due to language in the annual appropriations bill accompanying the program's funding.

[17] Section 473A(d)(3) of the Social Security Act. See also HHS, ACF, ACYF-CB-IM-09-03, September 1, 2009.

Table 1. Adoption Incentives: Summary of Appropriations and Award History

Appropriation Law	Appropriations	FY Adoptions Finalized	Award Amount
P.L. 105-277 (1999)	$19,994,999	FY1998 (35 states)	$42,510,000
P.L. 106-113 (2000)	$41,784,342	FY1999 (43 states and D.C.)	$51,488,000
P.L. 106-554 (2001)	$42,994,000	FY2000 (35 states and D.C.)	$33,238,000
P.L. 107-116 (2002)	$43,000,000	FY2001 (23 states and P.R.)	$17,578,000
P.L. 108-7 (2003)	$42,721,000[a]	FY2002 (25 states and P.R.)	$14,926,845
P.L. 108-199 (2004)	$7,456,000	FY2003 (31 states and P.R.)	$17,896,000
P.L. 108-447 (2005)	$9,346,000[b]	FY2004 (24 states, D.C. and P.R.)	$14,488,000
P.L. 109-149 (2006)	$17,808,000[a]	FY2005 (21 states)	$11,568,000
P.L. 110-7 (2007)	$5,000,000	FY2006 (19 states)	$7,354,000
P.L. 110-161 (2008)	$4,323,000	FY2007 (21 states)	$11,086,000
P.L. 111-8 (2009)	$36,500,000	FY2008 (38 states and D.C.)	$35,357,280[d]
P.L. 111-117 (2010)	$39,500,000	FY2009 (38 states and P.R.)	$45,896,000[d]
P.L. 112-10 (2011)	$39,421,000	FY2010 (32 states)	$40,144,000[a]
P.L. 112-74 (2012)	$39,346,000	FY2011 (30 states)	$36,472,000[c,d]
P.L. 113-6 (2013)	$39,346,000[e]	*Awards for FY2012 adoptions expected to be made in late FY2013.*	
TOTAL appropriated *(includes some funds transferred, lapsed, or subject to sequestration and therefore unavailable for award; see table notes)*	**$414,012,341**	**TOTAL expected to be awarded** *(includes amounts earned for FY2011 increases in numbers of adoptions for which funds were insufficient at the time of the initial award but which are expected to be paid)[c, d]*	**$379,858,125**

Source: Table prepared by the Congressional Research Service (CRS) based on appropriations laws, HHS, ACF budget justifications, and CRS communication with ACF budget and program analysts who work on Adoption Incentives.

a. Some of the funds provided in this appropriation cycle lapsed and were returned to the federal treasury. Funds may lapse when the Congressional authority for their use expires before they are needed to make incentive awards to states.

b. The appropriation in P.L. 108-447 was initially $31.8 million. However, as part of FY2006 appropriations (P.L. 109-149), Congress rescinded $22.5 million of that funding. In addition, HHS/ACF exercised its discretion to move 1% of the appropriated funds ($318,000) to the Refugee and Entrant Assistance program. This additionally reduced the total FY2005 funds available for Adoption Incentives to $9.0 million, although the amount shown in the table reflects funding after the rescission and prior to the transfer.

c. This is the total amount of funds states earned for increases in the numbers of adoptions finalized in FY2011. When it issued initial bonus funds for FY2011 adoptions (in August 2012), HHS had Adoption Incentive funding available to award 87% of this amount ($31.8 million). However, if HHS follows its past practice, states can expect to receive the remaining $4.7 million out of FY2013 program appropriations.

d. The award amounts shown in the final column of this table include increases tied to improved adoption rates only if those increases were paid to states. Beginning with adoptions finalized in FY2008-FY2011, states were eligible for increases in their Adoption Incentive awards if they improved their rate of adoptions. However, Section 473A(d)(3) of the Social Security Act provides that these awards may only be paid if funds remain available after any awards for increases in the *number* of adoptions are made. Funding was available to provide 48% ($1.7 million) of total increases ($3.5 million) calculated for improved FY2008 adoption rates. No funds were available to provide awards for any part of the increases for which states with improved adoption rates were eligible in FY2009 ($3.5 million), FY2010 ($2.3 million) or FY2011 ($0.9 million).

e. This appropriation is subject to the March 1 sequestration order, which is expected to reduce funding by 5%.

Awards by Category for Adoptions Finalized in FY2008-FY2011

Under the incentive structure used to make awards for adoptions finalized in FY2008-FY2011, states were eligible to receive $166 million and were expected to receive a total of $158 million in Adoption Incentive payments.

As of the end of FY2012, states had been paid 97% ($151 million) of the $156 million they earned for increasing the *numbers* of adoptions finalized in FY2008-FY2011. They are expected to receive the remaining 3% of the bonus amounts tied to increased number of adoptions, out of the FY2013 appropriation made for the Adoption Incentives program. By contrast, while states are *eligible* for increases in their adoption incentive payments when they improve on their highest-ever adoption rate, those additional incentive amounts may only be paid when the program funding exceeds what is needed to pay awards tied to increases in the number of adoptions. Therefore, although states were eligible for additional bonus payments of $10.2 million—for improving their adoption rates in award years FY2008-FY2011—they were paid only a fraction of that total (16% or $1.7 million) and no more of that total is to be paid.[18]

Under the current incentive structure, 44 states were paid Adoption Incentives bonus payments in one or more award category for adoptions finalized in any of FY2008-FY2011.[19] Among the eight states that were not paid an incentive for adoptions finalized in those years, five (Colorado, Massachusetts, New Jersey, Ohio, and Vermont) actually increased their *rate* of adoption in one or more of those award years and therefore were eligible for an adoption incentive payment, but did not receive an award due to the program funding level. Additionally, one state (New York) increased the number of special needs (under age 9) adoptions in three of those four years. However, because it did not earn an incentive in any of the other categories (foster child, older child, or adoption rate), it was not eligible for incentive funds for those increases. The remaining two states (District of Columbia and Iowa) did not increase the number of adoptions achieved or improve their rates of adoption in any of the four years.

Table 2 shows the total amounts paid (or expected to be paid) to states under the current incentive structure by award year and incentive category. States did not necessarily receive all of these bonus payments in a single fiscal year. Further, there were insufficient program funds available to pay bonuses for improved adoption rates in most years. Therefore the total amount of bonus payments that states were eligible to receive for adoptions finalized in FY2008-FY2011 is about $8 million more than the total amount they were expected to receive. (For incentive awards by category and for each state, see **Table D-5** in **Appendix D**.)

---

[18] Section 473A(d)(3) of the Social Security Act.

[19] For purposes of this discussion "states" are defined to include the 50 states, the District of Columbia and Puerto Rico, which makes a total of 52 states.

Table 2. Adoption Incentives for Adoptions Completed in FY2008–FY2011

Dollars in millions; summed parts may not equal totals due to rounding.

Incentive Category	FY2008	FY2009	FY2010	FY2011	Total
Foster Child	$16.1	$23.4	$18.9	$16.0	$74.5
Older Child (9 years or older)	$8.7	$12.0	$12.5	$11.8	$44.9
Special Needs (under 9 years)	$8.9	$10.3	$8.8	$8.7	$36.7
Adoption Rate	$3.5	$3.5	$2.3	$.09	$10.2
TOTAL incentives for which states were eligible[a]	*$37.1*	*$49.3*	*$42.4*	*$37.4*	*$166.3*
TOTAL incentives paid or expected to be paid[b]	**$35.4**	**$45.8**	**$40.1**	**$36.5**	**$157.7**

Source: Table prepared by the Congressional Research Service (CRS) based on data provided by HHS, Children's Bureau.

a. Beginning with FY2008, states are eligible for additional incentive sums based on improvements to their adoption rate *if sufficient appropriations are available to pay these awards after awards are made for increases in the numbers of adoptions.* FY2008 was the only year for which some funds were available for increases due to states' improved adoption rates. Eligible states were paid $1.7 million or about 48% of the $3.5 million in incentive amounts tied to improved adoption rates achieved that year. There were no funds available for incentives tied to adoption rate improvements in FY2009 ($3.5 million), FY2010 ($2.3 million), and FY2011 ($898,000).

b. Adoption Incentive awards are typically made at the end of the fiscal year for adoptions finalized in the previous fiscal year and after any unpaid awards tied to increases in the *number* of adoptions finalized in an earlier year. For example, HHS used FY2012 adoption incentive appropriations to complete bonus payments to states for increases in the number of adoptions finalized in FY2010. After those payments were made there was just $31.8 million remaining available from the FY2012 appropriations to make awards for adoptions finalized in FY2011. States received that amount (on a pro-rated basis) in August 2012. However, assuming HHS follows past practice, states are expected to be paid an additional $4.7 million (i.e., the remaining bonus amounts tied to increases in the *number* of adoptions finalized in FY2011) out of the FY2013 Adoption Incentives appropriations (and before any awards for adoptions finalized in FY2012 are made with those funds).

Foster Child Adoptions

States earned bonus payments of $74.5 million (45% of the total bonuses they were eligible to receive) for increasing their number of foster child adoptions finalized in FY2008-FY2011. That award category is the broadest—applying to children adopted from foster care generally. States may earn $4,000 for every adoption of a foster child in the given award year that is above the number of foster child adoptions the state completed in FY2007 (the baseline year). Sixteen states finalized more foster child adoptions in each of FY2008-FY2011 than they did in FY2007, and they earned foster child adoption bonuses in each of these four years. Half of the states (26) earned incentives for increases in foster child adoptions in at least one of the four years, and 10 states did not improve on their FY2007 record in any of these four years. (For information by state see **Table D-1** in **Appendix D**.)

Older Child Adoptions

Twenty-seven percent ($44.9 million) of the total bonus dollars states were eligible to receive for adoptions finalized in FY2008-FY2011 were tied to increases in the number of children who were adopted at 9 years of age or older. Adoptions of older children are less common than are adoptions of those who are younger. However, states may earn the largest award amount for increases in this incentive category. Specifically, states may earn $8,000 for every adoption of an "older child" in the given award year that is above the number of older child adoptions the state completed in FY2007 (the baseline year). Fifteen states earned incentives for increasing their numbers of older child adoptions in each of FY2008-FY2011 and close to half of the states (25) did so in at least one of those four years. Twelve states did not increase their number of older child adoptions (above their FY2007 level in the state) in any of those four years. (For information by state see **Table D-2** in **Appendix D**.)

Special Needs (Under Age 9) Adoptions

Twenty-two percent ($36.7 million) of the bonus funds states were eligible to receive for adoptions finalized in FY2008-FY2011 were linked to increases in the number of adoptions of children who were determined to have special needs and who were under the age of nine. States are only eligible to earn bonus funds in this category if they have earned an award in at least one other incentive category during the same fiscal year (i.e., they increased older child or foster child adoptions or they improved their rate of adoption). For eligible states, the award amount is $4,000 for every adoption of a special needs child under 9 years of age that is above the state's baseline number of such adoptions (i.e., above the number of such adoptions it achieved in FY2007).

For adoptions finalized in FY2008-FY2011, ten states increased their number of special needs (under age 9) adoptions above their baseline, but were not eligible in one or more years when this occurred because they did not earn a bonus in any other Adoption Incentive category in that same year. Overall, ten states earned bonus funds for increases in the number of special needs (under age 9) adoptions finalized in each of FY2008-FY2011; close to half of the states (24) did so in at least one of the four years; and 18 states did not earn an award in this category in any of those four years (either because they didn't increase the number of these adoptions or because they did not earn an incentive in any other award category). (For information by state see **Table D-3** in **Appendix D**.)

Adoption Rate

Finally, the total bonus amount a state is eligible to receive in a year is increased if the state improves its rate of adoption. However, this increased bonus amount is only authorized to be paid to states if sufficient appropriations remain available *after* awards are made for increases in the number of adoptions. For adoptions finalized in FY2008-FY2011, states were eligible for $10.2 million in bonus payments for improved adoption rates (6% of bonus payments states were eligible for across all four award categories). However, there were sufficient appropriations to award just $1.7 million of this amount.

A state's adoption rate is equal to the total number of foster child adoptions it completed in the fiscal year for every 100 children that were in its foster care caseload on the last day of the preceding fiscal year. An award for an increased rate of adoption can ensure that an incentive may be earned by a state that continues to appropriately move children from foster care to adoption even as the total number of children in foster care declines. In those states, the total number of children for whom adoption is the desired or appropriate permanency outcome is also likely to decline.

To be counted as having an improved adoption rate, a state was required to exceed the highest rate of adoptions it had achieved in any year (beginning with FY2002) that came before the year for which the awards were being calculated. A state that improved its adoption rate was eligible for $1,000 award for each adoption calculated to have been achieved due to the higher rate of adoptions.

The large majority of states (43) improved on their initial adoption rate baseline in one or more years from FY2008-FY2011. In FY2008, on average, states finalized roughly 11 adoptions for every 100 children who were in foster care; the comparable number for FY2011 was approaching 13 adoptions for every 100 children in foster care. (For information by state see **Table D-4** in **Appendix D**.)

Spending Award Money

States may spend Adoption Incentive funds anytime within a 24-month period, beginning with the month in which the funds are awarded to a state.[20] The statute permits states to spend these bonus dollars on any service authorized to be provided to children and families under Title IV-B or Title IV-E of the Social Security Act. Those parts of the law authorize a broad range of child welfare-related activities, including activities to prevent child abuse or neglect and/or provide services to enable a child to remain in his/her own home; investigation of alleged child abuse or neglect and placement of children in foster care if necessary; provision of services to reunite a child in foster care with his/her parents and for services to maintain the reunification; finding a new permanent home for children who may not be reunited with their parents, including through adoption or guardianship; provision of post-permanency services; and services to assist a youth in foster care to make a successful transition to adulthood. A state may not count its spending of Adoption Incentive funds toward meeting any of the "matching" requirements included in the programs authorized in Title IV-E and Title IV-B of the Social Security Act. (Programs under those parts of the law generally require states to supply between 20% -50% of the total program funding out of its non-federal, state or local, dollars.)[21]

Many states report spending incentive funds on adoption-related purposes, including post-adoption support services (e.g., support for adoptive parent mentors or adoptive family support groups, respite care, casework and supports for adoptive families of children at risk of re-entering foster care); recruitment of adoptive homes (e.g., support for online adoption exchange or photo-listing, development of promotional materials, child-specific recruitment efforts); and training or conferences to improve adoption casework. Other adoption-related services or supports funded with Adoption Incentive awards (in a smaller number of states) included provision of monthly adoption assistance payments, purchase of new equipment or provision of other resources to improve processing and archiving of adoption records, support for new or improved adoption home studies, and attention to inter-jurisdictional adoption placement. Some states used Adoption Incentive funds for foster care-related activities (e.g., training or recruitment of foster parents—alone or in combination with adoptive parents and foster and/or adoptive parent supports). Others referenced support for permanency efforts more generally (i.e., incorporating guardianship or reunification). At least one state reported using these incentive funds for foster care maintenance payments. Finally, a few states described use of Adoption Incentive funds for services to families

---

[20] Section 473A(e) of the Social Security Act. The 2008 reauthorization amended the law to ensure that states have a full two years from the date they receive the bonus funds to spend them. Prior law permitted states to spend funds through the end of the fiscal year following the fiscal year in which awards were made. However, because the bulk of award funding is provided in the waning days of the fiscal year, this typically permitted states only a little more than 12 months to spend the award funds.

[21] Section 473A(f) of the Social Security Act.

and children remaining in the home (e.g., alternative response and direct child protection services).[22]

Selected Reauthorization Issues

From its inception in 1997, the Adoption Incentives program has sought to encourage permanency for more children by rewarding states that increase the number of adoptions of children who would otherwise have no permanent family to call their own. In considering its reauthorization Congress may want to examine the continued need for and purpose of incentives for adoption, as well as, the particular focus and structure of any continued program. Selected issues are discussed below.

Continued Need For and Focus of Incentives

Since the 1997 enactment of ASFA, including the Adoption Incentives program, the number and rate of adoptions from foster care has increased significantly and the length of time needed to complete those adoptions has decreased. Given these successes, Congress might consider whether there is a continued need for this incentive program. On the other hand—given that each year many more children remain in foster care waiting for adoptions than are adopted, and also that many thousands of youth age out of state custody (26,000 in FY2011) without being safely reunited with biological parents or placed in a new permanent family—Congress may seek to continue the program with adjustments. For example, Congress could provide incentives to states for successful exits from foster care to permanent families of any kind (e.g., safe return to biological family and/or legal guardianship with a family, in addition to adoption). Alternatively, Congress could continue to exclusively support exits to adoption but it could refocus the kinds of categories for which states receive awards. For example, Congress could limit awards to successful adoption of the hardest to place children exclusively, such as older youth (particularly those entering care at an older age), children or youth with multiple foster care placements, or those with mental health challenges.

Permanence for Older Children

Youth who leave foster care without placement in a permanent family are at high-risk for homelessness, poor job outcomes, low educational attainment, and other negative outcomes.[23] Beginning with adoptions finalized in FY2004, the Adoption Incentives program offered states particular incentives for the adoption of children who are age 9 or older. These children are referred to as "older" in the Adoption Incentives program. Despite this incentive, older child adoptions remain less common than those of younger children. Among children adopted from foster care, 31% were age nine or older in FY2004 and in FY2011 that share was just 26%. In addition, many older children continue to leave foster care without placement in a permanent family. Among youth who left foster care in FY2004 and were age 15 or older, 21,600 were

---

[22] Based on CRS review of state Annual Progress and Services Reports (APSRs) submitted by states, generally, in mid- to late-2012, as part of requesting certain federal FY2013 child welfare funding.

[23] See CRS Report R40218, *Youth Transitioning from Foster Care: Issues for Congress*, by Adrienne L. Fernandes-Alcantara.

emancipated and an additional 4,200 were formally discharged with an exit reason of "runaway." The comparable figures in FY2011 were 24,300 and 1,300.

Congress may consider ways to further adjust the incentive structure or make other changes designed to reduce the number of youth who leave care without placement in a permanent family. As discussed by witnesses at a February 27, 2013 hearing held by the Subcommittee on Human Resources of the House Ways and Means Committee, ensuring adoption (or permanence via guardianship) is possible but may require specific kinds of recruitment efforts, youth engagement in the process, belief on the part of caseworkers that permanence can be achieved for these youth and more limited or different use of the case plan goal "another planned permanent living arrangement (APPLA)" for older youth. (For more discussion see "Related Legislative Actions in the 113th Congress.")

Baseline Adjustment

Congress may consider whether to adjust the baselines used to determine whether a state has achieved an increase in the number of foster child, older child, or special needs under age 9 adoptions. Throughout the program history, the incentive structure has been adjusted by Congress to update the award structure to ensure continued incentive for states to increase adoptions from foster care. (See **Appendix C**.)

Currently states must achieve a higher number of adoptions than they achieved in FY2007 to be eligible for awards in the foster child, older child, or special needs under age 9 award categories. Nationally, between FY2007 and FY2011, the number of children in foster care declined by 18% (from 510,000 to 401,000) and the number of those children in foster care who were counted as "waiting for adoption" declined by 22% (from 134,000 to 104,000).[24] While the amount and kind of change in the foster child and "waiting" population varied greatly by state, only six states saw an increase in their foster care caseload from the last day of FY2007 to the last day of FY2011 and just eight saw an increase in the number of children waiting for adoption. (See **Table E-1** and **Table E-2** in **Appendix E**.)

A declining number of children for whom adoption is appropriate makes it more difficult to exceed an absolute number of adoptions that were achieved in a state when that number of children was larger. The 2008 reauthorization of the Adoption Incentives program sought to address this concern, in part, by moving the "baseline" year closer to the year for which the award is to be determined. Separately, it authorized some awards based on improved adoption rates as discussed below.

Availability of Awards for Improved Rate of Adoption

Calculating a state's rate of adoption—that is the number of foster child adoptions in a given year for every 100 children in foster care on the last day of the prior fiscal year—effectively holds

---

[24] There is no formal definition in federal law or regulation of children who are "waiting for adoption." In its published counts of children "waiting for adoption," HHS counts any child in foster care who has a case plan goal of adoption and/or (in most cases) children for whom all parental rights have been terminated. Youth who are age 16 or older and for whom all parental rights have been terminated are excluded from this count *if they* have a case plan goal of "emancipation."

constant the size of the state's foster care caseload and thus provides a view of a state's success at completing adoptions that is independent of any change in the size of its foster care caseload. Congress introduced this new award category as part of the FY2008 reauthorization of the Adoption Incentive Program. However, although nearly every state improved its rate of adoption since this award category was established (see **Table D-4** in **Appendix D**) only 1% of all bonus funds expected to be paid for adoptions in FY2008 through FY2011 were tied to adoption rate increases. The reasons for this include the following:

- The size of the award for a rate increase ($1,000), which is just one-quarter of the award amount offered for increases in the number of foster child or special needs under age 9 adoptions and one-eighth of the amount offered for older child adoptions.

- The stipulation that awards for adoption rate increases may only be paid once states receive all award amounts earned for an absolute increase in the *number* of children adopted. (There have been sufficient funds to pay just $1.7 million of the total $10.2 million in increased bonuses states were eligible for due to rate increases since this award category was established.)

- The fact that the baseline for this award category changes to a higher rate each year the state makes an improvement in its adoption rate. (By contrast, the baselines for increases in each of the number of adoption award categories are fixed at the state's level of success in FY2007.)

Use of Incentive Funds

States may spend Adoption Incentive funds they receive for any of the range of child welfare services authorized under Title IV-B or Title IV-E of the Social Security Act and they may not count these funds as "non-federal" dollars for purposes of providing required matching dollars under any of those programs. The Administration, as part of its FY2014 budget request for reauthorization of the Adoption Incentive program, proposes requiring states to spend any of these bonus funds on "trauma-informed services to improve social and emotional well-being of children waiting for adoption or those having achieved adoption."[25] Congress might consider narrowing the purposes on which states might spend incentive funds. For example, they might limit use of the awards to post-permanency-related supports or to the trauma-informed services proposed by the Administration. Additionally, or alone, they might stipulate certain activities that may not be supported with these funds (e.g., foster care maintenance, adoption assistance, or guardianship assistance payments). On the other hand, given that bonus funds are by their nature less predictable than other kinds of federal grants, and the fact that states have earned the bonus by improved performance, Congress might choose to retain the current flexibility states have in the use of these funds.

---

[25] U.S. Department of Health and Human Services (HHS), Administration for Children and Families (ACF), *FY2014 Justification of Estimates for Appropriations Committees,* April 2013, p. 152.

Related Legislative Actions in the 113th Congress

On February 27, 2013, the Subcommittee on Human Resources of the House Ways and Means Committee held a hearing on "Increasing Adoptions from Foster Care." Subcommittee Chairman Dave Reichert, noting the increase in adoptions and decline in the foster care caseload since the enactment of the Adoption Incentives program and other changes to the law in 1997, said that the hearing was to consider if other changes were needed to encourage adoption from foster care.[26] Four witnesses discussed the importance of adoption as a way for children to find permanent homes and they gave particular attention to the need for adoptions of older children and those with special needs. Each of the witnesses supported reauthorization of the Adoption Incentives program.

Several witnesses described successful efforts to recruit adoptive families for older or harder to place children as those that start with a focus on the individual children or youth in need of families and engage them in the search for those families.[27] One recruitment model, known as "Wendy's Wonderful Kids" includes small caseloads that allow adoption caseworkers to get to know and work with the children for whom they are seeking permanent homes. A rigorous study of the model's effectiveness found that children served under this recruitment and placement model were one and a half times more likely to leave foster care for permanent homes then those who received traditional adoptive home recruitment services. The model's impact is greatest among older children and those with mental health disorders.[28] The state of Ohio has recently contracted to use the Wendy's Wonderful Kids model (on a nearly statewide basis) to find homes for harder to place children age 9 or older. By moving children from foster care to permanent homes more quickly, Ohio anticipates significant fiscal savings.[29]

Raising awareness of the need for adoptive families is a central goal of the Wait No More campaign, discussed by another hearing witness. This campaign brings together public child welfare agencies, private and public adoption agencies, church leaders and other support partners to promote and host adoption events at churches around the country. Interested families may begin the adoption process at the event, where speakers stress that adoption is about meeting the needs of the child (not the needs of adults), discuss common behavioral challenges for adoptees from foster care, and, offer strategies to enable successful child and family outcomes.[30]

Witnesses also focused on the need for post-adoption services, including counselors with specific training and knowledge about the needs of adoptive families, to ensure safety and stability of these families.[31] One witness asked that the longer-standing federal focus and financial support

[26] See Opening Statement of Chairman Dave Reichert, Subcommittee on Human Resources of the House Ways and Means Committee, *Hearing on Increasing Adoptions from Foster Care*, February 27, 2013. (Hereafter *Hearing*, February 27, 2013.)

[27] Testimony of Rita Soronen, President and CEO, Dave Thomas Foundation for Adoption and Testimony of Pat O'Brien, Executive Director and Founder, You Gotta Believe! The Older Child Adoption and Permanency Movement, Inc., *Hearing*, February 27, 2013.

[28] Karin Malm, Sharon Vandivere, with Tiffany Allen, Kerry DeVooght, Raquel. Ellis, Amy McLindon, Jacqueline Smollar, Eric Williams, and Andrew Zinn, *Evaluation Report Summary: The Wendy's Wonderful Kids' Initiative*, Child Trends, Washington, D.C.: 2011, pp. 9-11, 14-15.

[29] Testimony of Rita Soronen, *Hearing*, February 27, 2013.

[30] Testimony of Kelly Rosati, Vice President, Community Outreach, Focus on the Family, *Hearing*, February 27, 2013.

[31] Ibid. See also Testimony of Nicole Dobbins, Executive Director, Voice for Adoption, *Hearing*, February 27, 2013.

for increasing adoptions be coupled with a greater focus on (and financial support for) post-adoption services and suggested that Congress require states to spend their Adoption Incentive funds on post-adoption support.[32] Another asked that Congress ensure that children who were adopted did not lose access to education, mental health-related or other services that would be available to them if they remained in foster care.[33]

Several witnesses mentioned assignment of the case plan goal "another planned permanent living arrangement" (APPLA) as a potential barrier to finding permanent families for youth in care.[34] Once a youth's goal is fixed as "APPLA," one witness noted the child welfare agency stops searching for a permanent family and focuses exclusively on preparing the youth for "independent living." He asserted that federal policy should always require efforts to find a permanent home for youth in care and noted that those efforts could continue even as the agency worked to help the youth develop independent living skills.[35]

Other issues raised at the hearing included a call for reauthorization of the separate competitive grant program known as Family Connections,[36, 37] which one witness noted supports projects that can help connect youth with permanent families through greater kinship support, intensive family-finding efforts and family group decision-making meetings, and greater use (by states) of Title IV-E training funds to support more competent adoption casework.[38] As part of the hearing question and answer, witnesses also supported expanding the Adoption Incentives program to reward states that help youth gain a safe, permanent family through means other than adoption. In particular, several mentioned the importance of legal guardianship to achieving a permanent family for some older youth.[39]

---

[32] Testimony of Nicole Dobbins. Dobbins also sought more accountability from states on their use of projected savings from the growing federal investment in Title IV-E adoption assistance (authorized by the Fostering Connections to Success and Increasing Adoptions Act, P.L. 110-351). She maintained that states should be required to invest a portion of any savings they experience (due to this increased federal adoption assistance support) in post-adoption support services.

[33] Testimony of Rosati, including response to questions at *Hearing*, February 27, 2013. While states may make certain benefits available only to youth who remain in care, Congress has provided that certain education benefits and other assistance available to youth who "age out" of care (under Title IV-E of the Social Security Act) may also be available to youth who leave foster care for adoption or guardianship on or after their 16th birthday. In addition, as part of the Higher Education Act, Congress permits any youth who was in foster care on or after his/her 13th birthday to apply for federal financial aid as an "independent" student. For more information, see CRS Report RL34499, *Youth Transitioning from Foster Care: Background and Federal Programs*, by Adrienne L. Fernandes-Alcantara.

[34] Testimony of Nicole Dobbins, Executive Director, Voice for Adoption and Testimony of Pat O'Brien, *Hearing*, February 27, 2013.

[35] Testimony of Pat O'Brien, *Hearing*, February 27, 2013.

[36] Family Connection grants were established in the Fostering Connections to Success and Increasing Adoptions Act (P.L. 110-351). That law placed the grant program in Section 427 of the Social Security Act and appropriated five years of funding for them ($15 million annually for FY2009-FY2013). In addition to family group decision-making meetings, intensive family-finding efforts, and kinship navigator programs, these competitive grants have also been available for support of residential family treatment. For more information see "Family Connection Grantees" on the website of the HHS, Children's Bureau-supported National Resource Center for Permanency and Family Connections.

[37] The President's FY2014 budget calls for extension of this grant program for two years (FY2014-FY2016). It also proposes integrating the use of trauma-informed and trauma-focused approaches and or services (into the existing program focus areas) and increasing access to services for children subject to the Indian Child Welfare Act (ICWA). HHS, ACF *FY2014 Justification of Estimates for Appropriations Committees*, April 2013, p. 341.

[38] Testimony of Nicole Dobbins, *Hearing*, February 27, 2013.

[39] See response of each witness to question raised by Representative Danny Davis, *Hearing*, February 27, 2013.

Appendix A. Glossary of Terms

ADOPTION RATE—The number of children in foster care who are adopted during a fiscal year for every 100 children who were in foster care on the last day of the previous fiscal year.

ADOPTION RATE BASELINE—Highest ever adoption rate achieved by the state for any fiscal year that is before the fiscal year for which the Adoption Incentive rate award is being determined, beginning with FY2002.

ANOTHER PLANNED PERMANENT LIVING ARRANGEMENT (APPLA)—Each child in foster care must have a permanency goal—that is a plan for leaving foster care to a permanent home. A hearing to determine (or re-determine) that permanency goal must be held no later than 12 months after a child enters foster care, and every 12 months thereafter while the child remains in foster care. If at this hearing it is determined that the child's plan for permanency may not be any of reuniting with his/her parents, placement for adoption, placement with a legal guardian, or going to live with a fit and willing relative, then a child's plan for exiting care may be "another planned permanent living arrangement."

BASELINE (as used in the Adoption Incentive program)—The standard against which state performance is measured to determine whether, in a given year, the state has increased its number of adoptions or improved its adoption rate. A baseline is specific to the state, and is based on a state's past performance. (The four specific baselines used in the current Adoption Incentives program are defined individually in this glossary.)

FOSTER CHILD ADOPTION—The finalized adoption of a child who, at the time of adoptive placement, was in public foster care under the placement and care responsibility of the state child welfare agency.

FOSTER CHILD ADOPTION BASELINE—The number of foster child adoptions in the state in FY2007 as reported by the state via the Adoption and Foster Care Analysis Reporting System (AFCARS).

GUARDIANSHIP—A judicially created legal relationship between child and caretaker which is intended to be permanent and self-sustaining as evidenced by the transfer to the caretaker of the following parental rights with respect to the child: protection, education, care and control of the person, custody of the person, and decision-making.

OLDER CHILD ADOPTION—The finalized adoption of a child who is nine years of age or older and who, at the time of the adoptive placement was in public foster care *or* was the subject of a Title IV-E adoption assistance agreement between the state child welfare agency and the child's adoptive parents.

OLDER CHILD ADOPTION BASELINE - The number of older child adoptions in the state in FY2007 as reported by the state via AFCARS.

SPECIAL NEEDS ADOPTION– The adoption of a child whom the state has determined (1) cannot be returned to his or her parents and (2) is unlikely to be adopted without assistance because of a particular factor or condition (e.g., child's age; membership in a sibling group; minority race/ethnicity; medical or physical condition; or emotional, mental or behavioral disability). Additionally, unless this is not in the best interest of the child, the state must have made reasonable efforts to place the child for adoption without providing assistance. (A state is required to enter into a Title IV-E adoption assistance agreement with the adoptive parents of any child it finds to have special needs.)

SPECIAL NEEDS (UNDER AGE 9) ADOPTION—The finalized adoption of a child who is eight years of age or younger and who at the time of the adoptive placement was the subject of a Title IV-E adoption assistance agreement between the state child welfare agency and the child's adoptive parents.

SPECIAL NEEDS (UNDER AGE 9) ADOPTION BASELINE—The number of special needs (under age 9) adoptions in the state in FY2007 as reported by the state via AFCARS.

TERMINATION OF PARENTAL RIGHTS (TPR)—The legal severing (in a state court /court of competent jurisdiction) of the parent-child relationship. (Typically this severs the rights and responsibilities of a biological parent to his/her child. In the case of a previously adopted child however, it is the severing of the rights and responsibilities of the adoptive parent.)

WAITING FOR ADOPTION (as counted by HHS, Children's Bureau)—A child who is in foster care and who has a case plan goal of adoption and/or to whom all parental rights have been terminated. Except that any youth age 16 or older and to whom all parental rights have been terminated is excluded *if* that youth has a case plan goal of "emancipation."

Appendix B. Trends in Adoptions with Public Child Welfare Agency Involvement

Table B-1 shows, by fiscal year, the number of adoptions in which the public child welfare agency was involved, the number of children in foster care (under the responsibility of the public child welfare agency) on the last day of the fiscal year, and the rate of adoptions. All children who leave public foster care for adoption are adopted with public child welfare agency involvement and they represent the very large number of children shown in the adoption column. A small number of children who do not enter foster care may also be adopted with public child welfare agency involvement and that number is also included in the number shown in the adoptions column.

Table B-1. Adoptions with Public Child Welfare Agency Involvement, FY1995-FY2011

Adoption Rate = Number of public child welfare agency adoptions in the given fiscal year for every 100 children in foster care on the last day of the preceding fiscal year.

Fiscal Year	Children in Public Foster Care *on the last day of the fiscal year*	Public Agency-Involved Adoptions *during the fiscal year*	Adoption Rate
1995	483,000	25,700	5.5
1996	507,000	27,800	5.7
1997	537,000	31,000	6.1
1998	559,000	38,000	7.1
1999	567,000	46,900	8.4
2000	552,000	51,100	9.0
2001	545,000	50,600	9.2
2002	523,000	51,400	9.4
2003	510,000	49,600	9.5
2004	508,000	51,000	10.0
2005	511,000	51,600	10.2
2006	505,000	50,600	9.9
2007	482,000	52,700	10.4
2008	464,000	55,200	11.5
2009	422,000	57,100	12.3
2010	406,000	53,600	12.7
2011	401,000	50,500	12.4

Source: Table prepared by the Congressional Research Service. Children in foster care based on Table 11-4, "Additional Tables and Figures," Chapter 11, U.S. House Ways and Means Committee, *2012, Green Book*. Adoptions (based on Table 11-56 in *2008 Green Book* (for FY2001 and earlier years) and HHS, Children's Bureau, "Adoptions of Children with Public Child Welfare Agency Involvement by State" posted in June 2011(for FY2002) and July 2012 (for FY2003-FY2012).

Note: Data are displayed rounded to nearest 1,000 for total caseload and nearest 100 for adoptions. However, whenever more exact numbers were available they were used to compute the rate shown.

Table B-2. Number of Children Waiting for Adoption and Percentage of Waiting Children Adopted, FY1998-FY2011

Fiscal Year	Children Waiting for Adoption *on last day of the fiscal year*	Percentage of Waiting Children Adopted *Children adopted in given fiscal year as percentage of waiting children on last day of previous fiscal year*
1998	125,000	*not available* a
1999	130,000	37%
2000	131,000	39%
2001	130,100	39%
2002	133,900	40%
2003	130,600	37%
2004	130,400	39%
2005	130,700	40%
2006	135,400	39%
2007	133,700	39%
2008	125,700	41%
2009	114,500	45%
2010	109,500	47%
2011	104,200	46%

Source: Table prepared by the Congressional Research Services based on data reported by states via AFCARS and provided to CRS by HHS, Children's Bureau.

Notes: Number of children waiting for adoption is displayed rounded to nearest 100. However, whenever a more exact number was available, it was used to calculate the percentage. There is no definition of "waiting children" in statute or regulation. For purposes of analysis, the HHS, Children's Bureau counts as "waiting" each child in foster care on the last day of the fiscal year who has a case plan goal of adoption and/or for whom all parental rights have been terminated. However, it *excludes* from this number any youth in care who is age 16 or older for whom all parental rights have been terminated if that youth's case plan goal is "emancipation."

a. Could not be calculated because there is no estimate of the number of waiting children in FY1997.

Table B-3. Average and Median Length of Time to Finalized Adoption, In Months, FY2000-FY2011

Fiscal Year	Months from Removal to Termination of Parental Rights (TPR) *(Among children later adopted)*		Months from Termination of Parental Rights (TPR) to Adoption		TOTAL TIME TO FINALIZE ADOPTION *Months from removal to adoption*	
	Average	*Median*	*Average*	*Median*	*Average*	*Median*
2000	32.3	26.0	15.9	12.0	45.9	39.3
2001	29.7	23.5	16.0	11.8	44.0	37.5
2002	27.8	21.5	16.1	12.0	42.9	35.9
2003	26.1	20.1	16.2	12.0	41.8	34.9
2004	24.4	19.3	15.8	11.3	40.3	33.5
2005	23.4	18.8	15.0	10.7	38.3	32.0
2006	22.3	18.4	14.6	10.5	36.9	31.1
2007	21.6	17.9	14.1	10.3	35.7	30.3
2008	21.0	17.7	14.3	10.5	35.2	30.2
2009	20.8	17.8	14.1	10.3	34.8	30.3
2010	20.6	17.7	13.8	10.0	34.6	30.0
2011	20.1	17.4	13.7	9.8	34.0	29.2

Source: Table prepared by the Congressional Research Service based on state-reported AFCARS data (as of August 2012) provided to CRS by HHS, Children's Bureau.

Note: The median length of time to adoption measures the point at which half of the children adopted in the given fiscal year reached a finalized adoption in fewer months and half in more. By contrast, an average combines the total months to adoptions for all children with a finalized adoption in the given fiscal year and divides that number by the total number of adoptions. The average time to adoption is considerably longer than the median time to adoption because the average is affected by children with significantly longer stays in foster care.

Appendix C. Adoption Incentive Bonus Structure

At each reauthorization of the Adoption Incentives program, Congress has adjusted the bonus structure. New award categories and adjustments to the baselines have placed greater emphasis on adoption of harder to place children, helped to ensure that earning an incentive was possible even as caseloads declined, and protected the value of the incentives from erosion by inflation.

Table C-1. Evolution of Adoption Incentives Bonus Structure

NA = not authorized

Bonus Structure	Original Structure *Adoption and Safe Families Act of 1997, P.L. 105-89*	Initial Amendment *Adoption Promotion Act of 2003, P.L. 108-145*	Current Structure *Fostering Connections and Increasing Adoptions Act of 2008, P.L. 110-351*
Award category	**Foster Child:** Increase in number of children adopted from foster care.	**Foster Child:** Same as prior law.	**Foster Child:** Same as prior law.
	Special Needs: Increase in number of children adopted who are determined to have "special needs."	**Special Needs Under Age 9:** Increase in number of children adopted who are determined to have special needs [b] and are younger than 9 years of age.	**Special Needs Under Age 9:** Same as prior law.
	NA	**Older Child:** Increase in number of older children (age 9 years or above) adopted.	**Older Child:** Same as prior law.
	NA	NA	**Adoption Rate:** Increase in rate of children adopted from foster care (where rate equals the state's number of foster child adoptions in a fiscal year for every 100 children in foster care in that state on the last day of the previous fiscal year).
Baselines Number	**Adoptions finalized in FY1998:** For each award category, the average number of adoptions achieved by the state in that category for FY1995-FY1997. **Adoptions finalized in FY1999-FY2002:** For each award category, the highest number of adoptions finalized by the state in that category in FY1997 or the highest number in any following fiscal year that precedes the year for which the award is being determined.	**Adoptions finalized in FY2003-FY2007:** For each award category, the highest number of adoptions finalized by the state in that category in FY2002 or the highest number in any following fiscal year that precedes the year for which the award is being determined.	**Adoptions finalized in FY2008-FY2012:** For each award category, the number of adoptions finalized by the state in that award category during FY2007.
Rate	NA	NA	**Adoptions finalized in FY2008-FY2012:** The highest rate of foster child adoptions achieved by the state in FY2002 or the highest rate achieved in any following fiscal year that precedes the year for which the award is being determined.

Bonus Structure	**Original Structure** *Adoption and Safe Families Act of 1997, P.L. 105-89*	**Initial Amendment** *Adoption Promotion Act of 2003, P.L. 108-145*	**Current Structure** *Fostering Connections and Increasing Adoptions Act of 2008, P.L. 110-351*
Bonus Amounts	**Foster Child:** $4,000 for every foster child adoption above the state's baseline.	**Foster Child:** Same as prior law.	**Foster Child:** Same as prior law.
	Special Needs: $2,000 for every special needs adoption above the state's baseline. (Except that a state may only earn a bonus in this category if it also earned a bonus for increases in foster child adoptions.)	**Special Needs under age 9:** $2,000 for every special needs under age nine adoption above the state's baseline. (Except that a state may only earn a bonus in this category if it also earned a bonus for increases in either foster child or older child adoptions.)	**Special Needs under age 9:** $4,000 for every special needs under age nine adoption above the state's baseline. (Except that a state may only earn a bonus in this category if it also earned a bonus for increases in either foster child or older child adoptions or if it improved its adoption rate.)
	NA	**Older Child:** $4,000 for every older child adoption above the state's baseline.	**Older Child:** $8,000 for every older child adoption above the state's baseline.
	NA	NA	**Adoption Rate:** $1,000 for every adoption finalized that is attributed to the state's higher rate of adoption. (States may only receive bonus funds in this award category if sufficient funds remain available to make the award after all bonuses have been paid for any increases in foster child, older child, and special needs under age 9 adoptions.)

Source: Table prepared by the Congressional Research Service.

Appendix D. Adoptions and Incentives Earned by Category and State

Table D-1. Foster Child Adoptions and Incentives Earned for FY2008-FY2011

Initial incentive awards are paid in the fiscal year following the year in which the incentive was earned

State	Baseline Number of Foster child adoptions in FY2007	Number of Foster Child Adoptions Finalized in				Incentives Earned for Foster Child Adoptions Finalized in			
		FY2008	FY2009	FY2010	FY2011	FY2008	FY2009	FY2010	FY2011
Alabama	349	402	624	606	439	$212,000	$1,100,000	$1,028,000	$360,000
Alaska	244	261	338	336	292	$68,000	$376,000	$368,000	$192,000
Arizona	1,565	1,596	1,636	2,045	2,243	$124,000	$284,000	$1,920,000	$2,712,000
Arkansas	401	498	591	589	589	$388,000	$760,000	$752,000	$752,000
California	7,622	7,777	7,033	5,644	5,007	$620,000	$0	$0	$0
Colorado	1,077	995	1,057	968	930	$0	$0	$0	$0
Connecticut	569	647	684	564	505	$312,000	$460,000	$0	$0
Delaware	118	111	125	67	95	$0	$28,000	$0	$0
District of Columbia	151	111	99	127	104	$0	$0	$0	$0
Florida	2,970	3,959	3,763	3,243	2,899	$3,956,000	$3,172,000	$1,092,000	$0
Georgia	1,237	1,265	1,242	1,193	1,060	$112,000	$20,000	$0	$0
Hawaii	242	257	265	209	192	$60,000	$92,000	$0	$0
Idaho	190	229	338	306	254	$156,000	$592,000	$464,000	$256,000
Illinois	1,512	1,527	1,414	1,214	482[a]	$60,000	$0	$0	$0
Indiana	1,278	1,506	1,562	1,458	1,554	$912,000	$1,136,000	$720,000	$1,104,000
Iowa	1,060	1,038	1,005	795	851	$0	$0	$0	$0
Kansas	777	704	863	685	777	$0	$344,000	$0	$0
Kentucky	689	779	842	754	824	$360,000	$612,000	$260,000	$540,000
Louisiana	419	587	576	638	641	$672,000	$628,000	$876,000	$888,000
Maine	329	322	336	274	291	$0	$28,000	$0	$0
Maryland	197	210	606	637	514	$52,000	$36,000	$160,000	$0
Massachusetts	794	712	790	726	724	$0	$0	$0	$0
Michigan	2,617	2,731	3,089	2,597	2,500	$456,000	$1,888,000	$0	$0
Minnesota	548	768	652	619	566	$880,000	$416,000	$284,000	$72,000
Mississippi	290	272	292	352	350	$0	$8,000	$248,000	$240,000
Missouri	896	956	1,009	954	1,048	$240,000	$452,000	$232,000	$608,000
Montana	245	238	185	181	234	$0	$0	$0	$0
Nebraska	483	537	575	424	408	$216,000	$368,000	$0	$0
Nevada	453	459	527	635	806	$24,000	$296,000	$728,000	$1,412,000
New Hampshire	141	167	136	173	144	$104,000	$0	$128,000	$12,000
New Jersey	1,561	1,255	1,349	1,282	1,084	$0	$0	$0	$0

State	Baseline *Number of Foster child adoptions in FY2007*	Number of Foster Child Adoptions Finalized in				Incentives Earned for Foster Child Adoptions Finalized in			
		FY2008	**FY2009**	**FY2010**	**FY2011**	**FY2008**	**FY2009**	**FY2010**	**FY2011**
New Mexico	*355*	427	437	420	351	$288,000	$328,000	$260,000	$0
New York	*2,488*	2,394	2,398	2,205	2,214	$0	$0	$0	$0
North Carolina	*1,521*	1,667	1,622	1,494	1,377	$584,000	$404,000	$0	$0
North Dakota	*125*	144	82	138	113	$76,000	$0	$52,000	$0
Ohio	*1,710*	1,505	1,453	1,359	1,420	$0	$0	$0	$0
Oklahoma	*1,227*	1,463	1,496	1,569	1,226	$944,000	$1,076,000	$1,368,000	$0
Oregon	*1,016*	1,050	1,101	780	652	$136,000	$340,000	$0	$0
Pennsylvania	*1,916*	2,082	2,234	2,362	1,999	$664,000	$1,272,000	$1,784,000	$332,000
Rhode Island	*239*	258	273	184	201	$76,000	$136,000	$0	$0
South Carolina	*431*	525	513	529	588	$376,000	$328,000	$392,000	$628,000
South Dakota	*160*	173	165	131	156	$52,000	$20,000	$0	$0
Tennessee	*1,214*	1,098	1,001	972	772	$0	$0	$0	$0
Texas	*4,022*	4,530	4,988	4,709	4,718	$2,032,000	$3,864,000	$2,748,000	$2,784,000
Utah	*450*	541	510	572	569	$364,000	$240,000	$488,000	$476,000
Vermont	*195*	181	156	161	134	$0	$0	$0	$0
Virginia	*668*	595	633	645	748	$0	$0	$0	$320,000
Washington	*1,276*	1,245	1,618	1,626	1,573	$0	$1,368,000	$1,400,000	$1,188,000
West Virginia	*398*	513	537	654	685	$460,000	$556,000	$1,024,000	$1,148,000
Wisconsin	*656*	624	725	690	644	$0	$276,000	$136,000	$0
Wyoming	*72*	82	69	69	73	$40,000	$0	$0	$4,000
Puerto Rico	*143*	133	179	98	42	$0	$144,000	$0	$0
TOTAL	*51,306*	*54,106*	*55,793*	*51,662*	*48,662*	*$16,076,00*	*$23,448,00*	*$18,912,000*	*$16,028,000*

Source: Table prepared by the Congressional Research Service based on earnings and award data received from HHS, Administration for Children and Families (ACF), Administration on Children, Youth, and Families (ACYF), Children's Bureau. Data shown for numbers of adoptions are as determined for the Adoption Incentives program and may differ somewhat from data reported elsewhere on adoptions with public child welfare agency involvement.

Note: For incentives earned in FY2009, FY2010 and FY2011, there were insufficient appropriations to pay the full bonus amounts earned at the time of the initial awards. Accordingly, for incentives earned in FY2009 and FY2010, states received a portion of their bonus amount at the time of the initial award (i.e., at the end of the fiscal year following the fiscal year in which the incentive was earned) and the remainder when sufficient funds were available (in the following fiscal year). For incentives earned for increases in the number of foster child adoptions finalized in FY2011, states received an initial, partial award in August 2012. However, assuming it follows past practice, HHS is expected to use Adoption Incentives funds appropriated for FY2013 to pay states the remaining incentive amounts for increases in foster child adoptions (up to the full amount shown in the final column of the table).

a. As part of its comments in *Child Welfare Outcomes, FY2008-FY2011*, Illinois notes it has begun an improvement plan to address certain data concerns, including recent system changes leading to a miscount of adoptions.

Table D-2. Older Child (Age 9 or Above) Adoptions and Incentives Earned, FY2008-FY2011

Initial incentive awards are paid in the fiscal year following the year in which the incentive was earned

State	Baseline Number of older child adoptions in FY2007	Number of Older Child Adoptions Finalized in				Incentives Earned for Older Child Adoptions Finalized in			
		FY2008	FY2009	FY2010	FY2011	FY2008	FY2009	FY2010	FY2011
Alabama	115	136	186	220	108	$168,000	$568,000	$840,000	$0
Alaska	72	87	99	114	89	$120,000	$216,000	$336,000	$136,000
Arizona	345	388	392	536	557	$344,000	$376,000	$1,528,000	$1,696,000
Arkansas	102	116	147	135	137	$112,000	$360,000	$264,000	$280,000
California	1,646	1,734	1,555	1,293	1,060	$704,000	$0	$0	$0
Colorado	236	207	204	210	207	$0	$0	$0	$0
Connecticut	140	157	156	142	126	$136,000	$128,000	$16,000	$0
Delaware	24	18	31	14	26	$0	$56,000	$0	$16,000
District of Columbia	63	38	36	49	40	$0	$0	$0	$0
Florida	703	951	919	843	771	$1,984,000	$1,728,000	$1,120,000	$544,000
Georgia	356	356	405	370	320	$0	$392,000	$112,000	$0
Hawaii	48	66	63	53	65	$144,000	$120,000	$40,000	$136,000
Idaho	56	60	92	83	80	$32,000	$288,000	$216,000	$192,000
Illinois	336	358	358	302	145[a]	$176,000	$176,000	$0	$0
Indiana	383	458	433	367	432	$600,000	$400,000	$0	$392,000
Iowa	240	213	217	179	163	$0	$0	$0	$0
Kansas	205	214	208	168	224	$72,000	$24,000	$0	$152,000
Kentucky	209	247	290	293	275	$304,000	$648,000	$672,000	$528,000
Louisiana	96	117	103	140	137	$168,000	$56,000	$352,000	$328,000
Maine	113	93	83	62	63	$0	$0	$0	$0
Maryland	43	61	170	167	140	$144,000	$160,000	$136,000	$0
Massachusetts	189	125	137	141	149	$0	$0	$0	$0
Michigan	828	843	963	758	694	$120,000	$1,080,000	$0	$0
Minnesota	153	158	158	162	148	$40,000	$40,000	$72,000	$0
Mississippi	95	84	86	91	111	$0	$0	$0	$128,000
Missouri	286	317	292	291	261	$248,000	$48,000	$40,000	$0
Montana	70	61	49	46	75	$0	$0	$0	$40,000
Nebraska	141	150	139	104	100	$72,000	$0	$0	$0
Nevada	122	122	111	153	223	$0	$0	$248,000	$808,000
New Hampshire	43	55	50	59	38	$96,000	$56,000	$128,000	$0
New Jersey	375	311	361	366	279	$0	$0	$0	$0
New Mexico	118	127	156	119	130	$72,000	$304,000	$8,000	$96,000
New York	1,053	976	952	798	803	$0	$0	$0	$0

State	Baseline Number of older child adoptions in FY2007	Number of Older Child Adoptions Finalized in				Incentives Earned for Older Child Adoptions Finalized in			
		FY2008	FY2009	FY2010	FY2011	FY2008	FY2009	FY2010	FY2011
North Carolina	376	438	455	460	408	$496,000	$632,000	$672,000	$256,000
North Dakota	27	26	24	37	29	$0	$0	$80,000	$16,000
Ohio	541	454	396	325	403	$0	$0	$0	$0
Oklahoma	343	376	350	381	320	$264,000	$56,000	$304,000	$0
Oregon	234	227	250	154	133	$0	$128,000	$0	$0
Pennsylvania	538	516	501	554	459	$0	$0	$128,000	$0
Rhode Island	57	64	63	44	54	$56,000	$48,000	$0	$0
South Carolina	113	135	125	126	150	$176,000	$96,000	$104,000	$296,000
South Dakota	51	38	42	36	41	$0	$0	$0	$0
Tennessee	524	435	342	379	276	$0	$0	$0	$0
Texas	805	1,007	1,122	1,172	1,246	$1,616,000	$2,536,000	$2,936,000	$3,528,000
Utah	80	93	83	105	106	$104,000	$24,000	$200,000	$208,000
Vermont	67	50	50	54	37	$0	$0	$0	$0
Virginia	215	164	217	224	294	$0	$16,000	$72,000	$632,000
Washington	246	240	307	392	332	$0	$488,000	$1,168,000	$688,000
West Virginia	105	107	153	183	179	$16,000	$384,000	$624,000	$592,000
Wisconsin	219	175	187	178	152	$0	$0	$0	$0
Wyoming	12	23	19	18	20	$88,000	$56,000	$48,000	$64,000
Puerto Rico	34	36	70	28	11	$16,000	$288,000	$0	$0
TOTAL	13,591	14,008	14,357	13,678	12,826	$8,688,00	$11,976,000	$12,464,000	$11,752,000

Source: Table prepared by the Congressional Research Service based on earnings and award data received from HHS, Administration for Children and Families (ACF), Administration on Children, Youth, and Families (ACYF), Children's Bureau. Data shown for numbers of adoptions are as determined for the Adoption Incentives program and may differ somewhat from data reported elsewhere on adoptions with public child welfare agency involvement.

Note: For incentives earned in FY2009, FY2010 and FY2011, there were insufficient appropriations to pay the full bonus amounts earned at the time of the initial awards. Accordingly, for incentives earned in FY2009 and FY2010, states received a portion of their bonus amount at the time of the initial award (i.e., at the end of the fiscal year following the fiscal year in which the incentive was earned) and the remainder when sufficient funds were available (in the following fiscal year). For incentives earned for increases in the number of older child adoptions finalized in FY2011, states received an initial, partial award in August 2012. However, assuming it follows past practice, HHS is expected to use Adoption Incentives funds appropriated for FY2013 to pay states the remaining incentive amounts for increases in older child adoptions (up to the full amount shown in the final column of the table).

a. As part of its comments in *Child Welfare Outcomes, FY2008-FY2011*, Illinois notes it has begun an improvement plan to address certain data concerns, including recent system changes leading to a miscount of adoptions.

Table D-3. Special Needs (Under Age 9) Adoptions and Incentives Earned, FY2008-FY2011

Initial incentive awards are paid in the fiscal year following the year in which the incentive was earned

State	Baseline Number of Special Needs (under 9) Adoptions in FY2007	Number of Special Needs (under age 9) Adoptions Finalized in				Incentives Earned for Special Needs (under age 9) Adoptions Finalized in			
		FY2008	FY2009	FY2010	FY2011	FY2008	FY2009	FY2010	FY2011
Alabama	110	118	20	6	58	$32,000	$0	$0	$0
Alaska	127	136	182	160	146	$36,000	$220,000	$132,000	$76,000
Arizona	1,026	989	973	1,180	1,388	$0	$0	$616,000	$1,448,000
Arkansas	181	256	285	320	289	$300,000	$416,000	$556,000	$432,000
California	4,921	4,884	4,539	3,735	3,248	$0	$0	$0	$0
Colorado	356	96	332	300	310	$0	$0	$0	$0
Connecticut	310	282	270	237	167	$0	$0	$0	$0
Delaware [a]	19	35	27	18	20	$0	$32,000	$0	$4,000
District of Columbia	52	38	12	0	44	$0	$0	$0	$0
Florida	1,181	1,994	1,570	1,589	1,543	$3,252,000	$1,556,000	$1,632,000	$1,448,000
Georgia	459	489	453	434	446	$120,000	$0	$0	$0
Hawaii	170	164	161	116	96	$0	$0	$0	$0
Idaho	106	147	210	198	155	$164,000	$416,000	$368,000	$196,000
Illinois [a]	0	0	462	670	253 [b]	$0	$0	$0	$0
Indiana	708	601	623	809	675	$0	$0	$404,000	$0
Iowa [a]	399	424	384	299	346	$0	$0	$0	$0
Kansas	396	343	454	369	394	$0	$232,000	$0	$0
Kentucky	464	489	536	445	527	$100,000	$288,000	$0	$252,000
Louisiana	210	299	323	342	324	$356,000	$452,000	$528,000	$456,000
Maine [a]	137	154	162	143	159	$68,000	$100,000	$0	$88,000
Maryland	23	0	82	294	86	$0	$0	$0	$0
Massachusetts	320	205	268	209	220	$0	$0	$0	$0
Michigan	1,027	1,097	1,276	831	46	$280,000	$996,000	$0	$0
Minnesota	231	323	243	191	228	$368,000	$48,000	$0	$0
Mississippi	149	149	158	199	192	$0	$36,000	$200,000	$172,000
Missouri	521	398	540	571	646	$0	$76,000	$200,000	$500,000
Montana	142	139	91	83	81	$0	$0	$0	$0
Nebraska [a]	114	175	202	168	157	$244,000	$352,000	$0	$0
Nevada	288	285	346	378	450	$0	$232,000	$360,000	$648,000
New Hampshire	87	103	68	86	71	$64,000	$0	$0	$0
New Jersey	885	242	577	578	459	$0	$0	$0	$0
New Mexico	207	245	235	249	173	$152,000	$112,000	$168,000	$0
New York [a]	969	1,022	1,082	1,071	924	$0	$0	$0	$0

State	Baseline Number of Special Needs (under 9) Adoptions in FY2007	Number of Special Needs (under age 9) Adoptions Finalized in				Incentives Earned for Special Needs (under age 9) Adoptions Finalized in			
		FY2008	FY2009	FY2010	FY2011	FY2008	FY2009	FY2010	FY2011
North Carolina	757	812	802	768	744	$220,000	$180,000	$44,000	$0
North Dakota	60	49	29	39	51	$0	$0	$0	$0
Ohio	1,135	919	880	890	903	$0	$0	$0	$0
Oklahoma	609	683	666	649	548	$296,000	$228,000	$160,000	$0
Oregon	615	636	678	481	443	$84,000	$252,000	$0	$0
Pennsylvania	1,099	1,232	1,395	1,413	1,253	$532,000	$1,184,000	$1,256,000	$616,000
Rhode Island	118	137	128	81	102	$76,000	$40,000	$0	$0
South Carolina	163	198	242	181	241	$140,000	$316,000	$72,000	$312,000
South Dakota [a]	75	89	87	69	88	$56,000	$48,000	$0	$0
Tennessee [a]	196	334	311	249	282	$552,000	$0	$212,000	$0
Texas	2,214	2,471	2,722	2,566	2,617	$1,028,000	$2,032,000	$1,408,000	$1,612,000
Utah	149	229	205	174	193	$320,000	$224,000	$100,000	$176,000
Vermont [a]	85	88	51	80	56	$0	$0	$0	$0
Virginia	327	309	282	271	290	$0	$0	$0	$0
Washington	975	936	576	938	935	$0	$0	$0	$0
West Virginia	244	252	300	332	308	$32,000	$224,000	$352,000	$256,000
Wisconsin [a]	422	402	431	410	439	$0	$36,000	$0	$0
Wyoming	31	27	22	19	9	$0	$0	$0	$0
Puerto Rico	36	45	34	28	8	$36,000	$0	$0	$0
TOTAL	25,605	26,169	26,987	25,916	23,831	$8,908,000	$10,328,000	$8,768,000	$8,692,000

Source: Table prepared by the Congressional Research Service based on earnings and award data received from HHS, Administration for Children and Families (ACF), Administration on Children, Youth, and Families (ACYF), Children's Bureau. Data shown for numbers of adoptions are as determined for the Adoption Incentives program and may differ somewhat from data reported elsewhere on adoptions with public child welfare agency involvement.

Note: For incentives earned in FY2009, FY2010 and FY2011, there were insufficient appropriations to pay the full bonus amounts earned at the time of the initial awards. Accordingly, for incentives earned in FY2009 and FY2010, states received a portion of their bonus amount at the time of the initial award (i.e., at the end of the fiscal year following the fiscal year in which the incentive was earned) and the remainder when sufficient funds were available (in the following fiscal year). For incentives earned for increases in the number of special needs (under age 9) adoptions finalized in FY2011, states received an initial, partial award in August 2012. However, assuming it follows past practice, HHS is expected to use Adoption Incentives funds appropriated for FY2013 to pay states the remaining incentive amounts for increases in special needs (under age 9) adoptions (up to the full amount shown in the final column of the table).

a. As provided in the law, states that exceeded their special needs (under age 9) adoption baseline did not earn an incentive for this increase unless, in that same fiscal year, they separately earned an incentive for increases in foster child or older child adoptions, or if they improved their adoption rate.

b. As part of its comments in *Child Welfare Outcomes, FY2008-FY2011*, Illinois notes it has begun an improvement plan to address certain data concerns, including recent system changes leading to a miscount of adoptions.

Table D-4. Adoption Rates and Incentive Increases for Improved Adoption Rate

Adoption Rate = Number of foster child adoptions finalized in the fiscal year for every 100 children in foster care on the last day of the previous fiscal year.

State	Initial Baseline Highest adoption rate FY2002-F2007	Actual Adoption Rate Achieved				Current Baseline Highest adoption rate FY2002-FY2011	Fiscal Year Highest Adoption Rate Achieved	Incentive Increases States Were Eligible to Receive			
		FY2008	FY2009	FY2010	FY2011			FY2008	FY2009	FY2010	FY2011
Alabama	6.5	5.5	9.1	9.8	8.2	9.8	FY2010	$0	$177,000	$44,000	$0
Alaska	12.3	12.3	15.6	15.5	16.5	16.5	FY2011	$0	$71,000	$0	$17,000
Arizona	16.0	16.7	15.7	21.7	22.6	22.6	FY2011	$65,000	$0	$471,000	$88,000
Arkansas	12.5	13.8	16.8	16.1	15.7	16.8	FY2009	$46,000	$105,000	$0	$0
California	10.0	10.5	10.4	9.4	8.9	10.5	FY2008	$377,000	$0	$0	$0
Colorado	13.2	12.8	13.3	13.1	13.3	13.3	FY2009	$0	$11,000	$0	$0
Connecticut	8.9	11.2	12.7	11.8	11.3	12.7	FY2009	$132,000	$82,000	$0	$0
Delaware	13.0	9.6	13.3	8.2	12.9	13.3	FY2009	$0	$3,000	$0	$0
District of Columbia	12.2	5.1	4.5	6.0	5.0	12.2	FY2004	$0	$0	$0	$0
Florida	10.4	14.8	17.0	16.9	15.5	17.0	FY2009	$1,173,000	$479,000	$0	$0
Georgia	9.4	10.4	12.4	14.8	15.4	15.4	FY2011	$118,000	$204,000	$193,000	$40,000
Hawaii	14.7	13.2	16.3	14.4	15.6	16.3	FY2009	$0	$27,000	$0	$0
Idaho	11.7	12.2	19.6	21.2	17.4	21.2	FY2010	$10,000	$128,000	$23,000	$0
Illinois	12.9	8.5	7.9	7.1	2.7a	12.9	FY2002	$0	$0	$0	$0
Indiana	11.2	13.2	12.6	11.9	12.7	13.2	FY2008	$232,000	$0	$0	$0
Iowa	21.0	12.6	14.9	12.1	13.0	21.0	FY2003	$0	$0	$0	$0
Kansas	12.5	10.6	13.7	12.0	13.0	13.7	FY2009	$0	$75,000	$0	$0
Kentucky	12.5	11.1	11.7	11.0	11.8	12.5	FY2005	$0	$0	$0	$0
Louisiana	10.6	11.0	11.4	13.3	14.4	14.4	FY2011	$22,000	$19,000	$92,000	$49,000

State	Initial Baseline Highest adoption rate FY2002-F2007	Actual Adoption Rate Achieved				Current Baseline Highest adoption rate FY2002-FY2011	Fiscal Year Highest Adoption Rate Achieved	Incentive Increases States Were Eligible to Receive			
		FY2008	FY2009	FY2010	FY2011			FY2008	FY2009	FY2010	FY2011
Maine	15.8	16.3	18.0	16.6	18.8	18.8	FY2011	$11,000	$32,000	$0	$13,000
Maryland	7.3	2.1	7.8	9.0	8.4	9.0	FY2010	$0	$40,000	$86,000	$0
Massachusetts	7.2	6.8	7.6	7.5	8.1	8.1	FY2011	$0	$39,000	$0	$43,000
Michigan	13.6	13.1	15.3	14.7	15.2	15.3	FY2009	$0	$346,000	$0	$0
Minnesota	10.1	11.4	10.8	11.4	11.2	11.4	FY2008	$86,000	$0	$0	$0
Mississippi	9.9	8.2	8.9	10.6	9.8	10.6	FY2010	$0	$0	$23,000	$0
Missouri	11.1	9.7	10.0	11.1	10.6	11.1	FY2002	$0	$0	$0	$0
Montana	12.8	13.7	11.6	11.0	13.6	13.7	FY2008	$16,000	$0	$0	$0
Nebraska	7.8	9.1	10.3	7.9	7.6	10.3	FY2009	$79,000	$66,000	$0	$0
Nevada	9.8	9.1	10.5	13.3	16.8	16.8	FY2011	$0	$35,000	$133,000	$167,000
New Hampshire	12.3	15.4	13.2	18.6	17.2	18.6	FY2010	$34,000	$0	$30,000	$0
New Jersey	14.5	13.9	15.9	16.4	15.7	16.4	FY2010	$0	$115,000	$41,000	$0
New Mexico	15.7	17.6	19.7	21.1	18.8	21.1	FY2010	$47,000	$46,000	$28,000	$0
New York	10.8	8.0	8.1	7.9	8.3	10.8	FY2004	$0	$0	$0	$0
North Carolina	13.7	15.4	16.5	15.6	15.6	16.5	FY2009	$184,000	$106,000	$0	$0
North Dakota	10.7	11.4	6.6	11.4	10.5	11.4	FY2008	$9,000	$0	$0	$0
Ohio	11.2	8.8	10.6	11.1	11.9	11.9	FY2011	$0	$0	$0	$83,000
Oklahoma	12.9	12.4	14.1	18.0	15.6	18.0	FY2010	$0	$129,000	$341,000	$0
Oregon	12.4	11.0	12.2	9.0	7.2	12.4	FY2002	$0	$0	$0	$0
Pennsylvania	9.3	10.0	11.6	13.9	13.2	13.9	FY2010	$142,000	$312,000	$394,000	$0
Rhode Island	11.0	9.5	11.3	8.7	9.6	11.3	FY2009	$0	$8,000	$0	$0
South Carolina	9.0	10.2	10.3	10.7	13.1	13.1	FY2011	$62,000	$3,000	$20,000	$108,000

State	Initial Baseline Highest adoption rate FY2002-F2007	Actual Adoption Rate Achieved				Current Baseline Highest adoption rate FY2002-FY2011	Fiscal Year Highest Adoption Rate Achieved	Incentive Increases States Were Eligible to Receive			
		FY2008	FY2009	FY2010	FY2011			FY2008	FY2009	FY2010	FY2011
South Dakota	10.4	11.0	11.1	8.8	10.5	11.1	FY2009	$10,000	$2,000	$0	$0
Tennessee	14.1	14.2	13.9	14.5	11.5	14.5	FY2010	$5,000	$0	$17,000	$0
Texas	13.0	15.0	17.7	17.6	16.3	17.7	FY2009	$612,000	$765,000	$0	$0
Utah	21.6	19.8	18.8	20.7	19.7	21.6	FY2006	$0	$0	$0	$0
Vermont	15.0	13.8	13.0	15.2	14.4	15.2	FY2010	$0	$0	$2,000	$0
Virginia	8.7	8.0	8.9	10.9	13.8	13.8	FY2011	$0	$15,000	$117,000	$158,000
Washington	13.6	11.2	14.1	14.8	15.5	15.5	FY2011	$0	$53,000	$80,000	$73,000
West Virginia	10.9	11.6	12.2	15.4	16.7	16.7	FY2011	$32,000	$25,000	$137,000	$52,000
Wisconsin	14.3	8.4	9.8	10.2	9.8	14.3	FY2004	$0	$0	$0	$0
Wyoming	6.1	6.7	6.0	6.0	7.4	7.4	FY2011	$7,000	$0	$0	$7,000
Puerto Rico	2.7	2.0	2.9	1.8	0.9	2.9	FY2009	$0	$12,000	$0	$0
Median	*12.0*	11.2	12.2	12.0	13.1	*13.8*		$3,511,000	$3,530,000	$2,272,000	$898,000

Source: Table prepared by the Congressional Research Service based on earnings and award data received from HHS, Administration for Children and Families, Administration on Children, Youth, and Families, Children's Bureau. Adoption data used to calculate these rates are based on foster child adoptions as counted for the Adoption Incentives program.

Note: A state is eligible for an increase in its Adoption Incentive award (above the amount, if any, it earned for increases in number of adoptions) if it improves its adoption rate. However, any increase due to improved adoption rates may only be paid if there are sufficient funds remaining after the awards are made for increased *numbers* of adoption. FY2008 is the first year for which increases tied to improved adoption rates were authorized and it is also the only earnings year for which some funds were available to pay these increases. Specifically, for that year there were sufficient funds to pay about one-half (48%) of the increases for which states with improved adoption rates were eligible. (The full increase for which states were eligible is shown in the table above, although states received less than $1.7 million of these amounts.) In each succeeding earnings year, there were no funds available to pay increased incentive amounts to states with improved adoption rates. Therefore, none of the amounts shown in the table above (for FY2009, FY2010, or FY2011) were paid to states that improved their adoption rates in those years.

a. As part of its comments in *Child Welfare Outcomes, FY2008-FY2011*, Illinois notes it has begun an improvement plan to address certain data concerns, including recent system changes leading to a miscount of adoptions.

Table D-5. Incentives Earned by Award Category for Adoptions Finalized in FY2008-FY2011

Blank cell indicates not applicable

State	Foster Child		Older Child		Special Needs under Age 9		Adoption Rate		Total Incentive Amount for which State was Eligible	Adoption Rate Amount Paid		TOTAL Expected to Be Paid[a]
	$	%	$	%	$	%	$	%		$	%	
Alabama	$2,700,000	59.6%	$1,576,000	34.8%	$32,000	0.7%	$221,000	4.9%	$4,529,000	$0	0.0%	$4,308,000
Alaska	$1,004,000	42.5%	$808,000	34.2%	$464,000	19.6%	$88,000	3.7%	$2,364,000	$0	0.0%	$2,276,000
Arizona	$5,040,000	43.2%	$3,944,000	33.8%	$2,064,000	17.7%	$624,000	5.3%	$11,672,000	$31,200	5.0%	$11,079,200
Arkansas	$2,652,000	48.0%	$1,016,000	18.4%	$1,704,000	30.9%	$151,000	2.7%	$5,523,000	$22,080	14.6%	$5,394,080
California	$620,000	36.4%	$704,000	41.4%	$0	0.0%	$377,000	22.2%	$1,701,000	$180,960	48.0%	$1,504,960
Colorado	$0		$0	0.0%	$0	0.0%	$11,000	100.0%	$11,000	$0	0.0%	$0
Connecticut	$772,000	61.0%	$280,000	22.1%	$0	0.0%	$214,000	16.9%	$1,266,000	$63,360	29.6%	$1,115,360
Delaware	$28,000	20.1%	$72,000	51.8%	$36,000	25.9%	$3,000	2.2%	$139,000	$0	0.0%	$136,000
District of Columbia	$0		$0		$0		$0		$0			$0
Florida	$8,220,000	35.5%	$5,376,000	23.2%	$7,888,000	34.1%	$1,652,000	7.1%	$23,136,000	$563,040	34.1%	$22,047,040
Georgia	$132,000	10.1%	$504,000	38.4%	$120,000	9.2%	$555,000	42.3%	$1,311,000	$56,640	10.2%	$812,640
Hawaii	$152,000	24.6%	$440,000	71.1%	$0	0.0%	$27,000	4.4%	$619,000	$0	0.0%	$592,000
Idaho	$1,468,000	41.9%	$728,000	20.8%	$1,144,000	32.7%	$161,000	4.6%	$3,501,000	$4,800	3.0%	$3,344,800
Illinois	$60,000	14.6%	$352,000	85.4%	$0	0.0%	$0	0.0%	$412,000	$0		$412,000
Indiana	$3,872,000	65.6%	$1,392,000	23.6%	$404,000	6.8%	$232,000	3.9%	$5,900,000	$111,360	48.0%	$5,779,360
Iowa	$0		$0		$0		$0		$0			$0
Kansas	$344,000	38.3%	$248,000	27.6%	$232,000	25.8%	$75,000	8.3%	$899,000	$0	0.0%	$824,000
Kentucky	$1,772,000	38.8%	$2,152,000	47.2%	$640,000	14.0%	$0	0.0%	$4,564,000	$0	0.0%	$4,564,000
Louisiana	$3,064,000	51.6%	$904,000	15.2%	$1,792,000	30.2%	$182,000	3.1%	$5,942,000	$10,560	5.8%	$5,770,560

State	Foster Child		Older Child		Special Needs under Age 9		Adoption Rate		Total Incentive Amount for which State was Eligible	Adoption Rate Amount Paid		TOTAL Expected to Be Paid[a]
	$	%	$	%	$	%	$	%		$	%	
Maine	$28,000	8.2%	$0	0.0%	$256,000	75.3%	$56,000	16.5%	$340,000	$5,280	9.4%	$289,280
Maryland	$248,000	30.5%	$440,000	54.1%	$0	0.0%	$126,000	15.5%	$814,000	$0	0.0%	$688,000
Massachusetts	$0	0.0%	$0	0.0%	$0	0.0%	$82,000	100.0%	$82,000	$0	0.0%	$0
Michigan	$2,344,000	45.4%	$1,200,000	23.2%	$1,276,000	24.7%	$346,000	6.7%	$5,166,000	$0	0.0%	$4,820,000
Minnesota	$1,652,000	71.6%	$152,000	6.6%	$416,000	18.0%	$86,000	3.7%	$2,306,000	$41,280	48.0%	$2,261,280
Mississippi	$496,000	47.0%	$128,000	12.1%	$408,000	38.7%	$23,000	2.2%	$1,055,000	$0	0.0%	$1,032,000
Missouri	$1,532,000	57.9%	$336,000	12.7%	$776,000	29.3%	$0	0.0%	$2,644,000			$2,644,000
Montana	$0	0.0%	$40,000	71.4%	$0	0.0%	$16,000	28.6%	$56,000	$7,680	48.0%	$47,680
Nebraska	$584,000	41.8%	$72,000	5.2%	$596,000	42.7%	$145,000	10.4%	$1,397,000	$37,920	26.2%	$1,289,920
Nevada	$2,460,000	48.3%	$1,056,000	20.7%	$1,240,000	24.4%	$335,000	6.6%	$5,091,000	$0	0.0%	$4,756,000
New Hampshire	$244,000	37.4%	$280,000	42.9%	$64,000	9.8%	$64,000	9.8%	$652,000	$16,320	25.5%	$604,320
New Jersey	$0	0.0%	$0	0.0%	$0	0.0%	$156,000	100.0%	$156,000	$0	0.0%	$0
New Mexico	$876,000	45.9%	$480,000	25.1%	$432,000	22.6%	$121,000	6.3%	$1,909,000	$22,560	18.6%	$1,810,560
New York	$0	0.0%	$0	0.0%	$0	0.0%	$0		$0	$0	0.0%	$0
North Carolina	$988,000	26.2%	$2,056,000	54.4%	$444,000	11.8%	$290,000	7.7%	$3,778,000	$88,320	30.5%	$3,576,320
North Dakota	$128,000	54.9%	$96,000	41.2%	$0	0.0%	$9,000	3.9%	$233,000	$4,320	48.0%	$228,320
Ohio	$0	0.0%	$0	0.0%	$0	0.0%	$83,000	100.0%	$83,000	$0	0.0%	$0
Oklahoma	$3,388,000	65.6%	$624,000	12.1%	$684,000	13.2%	$470,000	9.1%	$5,166,000	$0	0.0%	$4,696,000
Oregon	$476,000	50.6%	$128,000	13.6%	$336,000	35.7%	$0	0.0%	$940,000			$940,000
Pennsylvania	$4,052,000	47.0%	$128,000	1.5%	$3,588,000	41.6%	$848,000	9.8%	$8,616,000	$68,160	8.0%	$7,836,160
Rhode Island	$212,000	48.2%	$104,000	23.6%	$116,000	26.4%	$8,000	1.8%	$440,000	$0	0.0%	$432,000

State	Foster Child		Older Child		Special Needs under Age 9		Adoption Rate		Total Incentive Amount for which State was Eligible	Adoption Rate Amount Paid		TOTAL Expected to Be Paid[a]
	$	%	$	%	$	%	$	%		$	%	
South Carolina	$1,724,000	50.3%	$672,000	19.6%	$840,000	24.5%	$193,000	5.6%	$3,429,000	$29,760	15.4%	$3,265,760
South Dakota	$72,000	38.3%	$0	0.0%	$104,000	55.3%	$12,000	6.4%	$188,000	$4,800	40.0%	$180,800
Tennessee	$0	0.0%	$0	0.0%	$764,000	97.2%	$22,000	2.8%	$786,000	$2,400	10.9%	$766,400
Texas	$11,428,000	38.7%	$10,616,000	36.0%	$6,080,000	20.6%	$1,377,000	4.7%	$29,501,000	$293,760	21.3%	$28,417,760
Utah	$1,568,000	53.6%	$536,000	18.3%	$820,000	28.0%	$0	0.0%	$2,924,000			$2,924,000
Vermont	$0	0.0%	$0	0.0%	$0	0.0%	$2,000	100.0%	$2,000	$0	0.0%	$0
Virginia	$320,000	24.1%	$720,000	54.1%	$0	0.0%	$290,000	21.8%	$1,330,000	$0	0.0%	$1,040,000
Washington	$3,956,000	60.8%	$2,344,000	36.0%	$0	0.0%	$206,000	3.2%	$6,506,000	$0	0.0%	$6,300,000
West Virginia	$3,188,000	53.9%	$1,616,000	27.3%	$864,000	14.6%	$246,000	4.2%	$5,914,000	$15,360	6.2%	$5,683,360
Wisconsin	$412,000	92.0%	$0	0.0%	$36,000	8.0%	$0	0.0%	$448,000	$448,000		$448,000
Wyoming	$44,000	14.0%	$256,000	81.5%	$0	0.0%	$14,000	4.5%	$314,000	$3,360	24.0%	$303,360
Puerto Rico	$144,000	29.0%	$304,000	61.3%	$36,000	7.3%	$12,000	2.4%	$496,000	$0	0.0%	$484,000
TOTAL	$74,464,000	44.8%	$44,880,000	27.0%	$36,696,000	22.1%	$10,211,000	6.1%	$166,251,000	$1,685,280	16.5%	$157,725,280

Source: Table prepared by the Congressional Research Service based on earnings and award data received from HHS, Administration for Children and Families (ACF), Administration on Children, Youth, and Families (ACYF), Children's Bureau.

Note: States are expected to receive all incentive amounts they were eligible to receive for increases in the number of foster child, older child, and special needs (under age 9) adoptions. However, they may only receive awards for improved adoption rates if there are sufficient funds to pay these awards at the time initial awards are made for a fiscal year and after all awards for increases in numbers of adoptions are made. There were sufficient funds to pay some (48%) of awards earned for improved adoption rates for adoptions finalized in FY2008. However, there were no funds for this award category for adoptions finalized in FY2009, FY2010, or FY2011.

a. In August 2012, states received an initial portion of any incentive earned for increases in the number of foster child, older child, or special needs (under age 9) adoptions. At that time there were insufficient funds to pay the full amount states earned. Therefore, states received a pro-rated amount ($31.8 million, 87%) of the award they were eligible for increases in numbers of adoptions. Assuming HHS follows past practice, however, states are expected to receive the remaining award amount ($4.7 million) out of FY2013 appropriations provided for the Adoption Incentive program.

Appendix E. Children in Foster Care and Waiting for Adoption by State

Table E-1. Children in Foster Care on the Last Day of the Fiscal Year by State, FY2007-FY2011

States are ordered by caseload change (largest % decline to greatest % increase), FY2007 to FY2011

State	FY2007	FY2008	FY2009	FY2010	FY2011	% Change in Caseload FY2007-FY2011
Hawaii	1,940	1,621	1,472	1,234	1,126	-42.0%
Georgia	12,197	9,984	8,068	6,895	7,591	-37.8%
Virginia	7,718	7,099	5,968	5,414	4,846	-37.2%
Rhode Island	2,768	2,407	2,112	2,086	1,806	-34.8%
Maine	1,971	1,864	1,646	1,546	1,296	-34.2%
New Hampshire	1,102	1,029	930	839	742	-32.7%
Pennsylvania	20,999	26,571	16,623	15,179	14,175	-32.5%
Maryland	8,415	7,613	7,065	6,098	5,704	-32.2%
Puerto Rico	6,330	6,185	5,351	4,476	4,363	-31.1%
Oklahoma	11,785	10,595	8,712	7,857	8,280	-29.7%
New Jersey	9,056	8,510	7,803	6,892	6,440	-28.9%
Wyoming	1,231	1,154	1,155	981	886	-28.0%
Idaho	1,870	1,723	1,446	1,462	1,354	-27.6%
Michigan	20,830	20,171	17,723	16,412	15,105	-27.5%
Alabama	7,262	6,941	6,179	5,350	5,295	-27.1%
Delaware	1,157	938	814	739	845	-27.0%
Florida	26,788	22,187	19,162	18,743	19,760	-26.2%
South Carolina	5,167	5,054	4,978	4,487	3,821	-26.0%
Minnesota	6,711	6,028	5,410	5,050	4,995	-25.6%
California	73,998	67,703	60,583	56,183	55,409	-25.1%
New Mexico	2,423	2,221	1,992	1,869	1,859	-23.3%
Vermont	1,309	1,200	1,062	933	1,010	-22.8%
Iowa	8,005	6,743	6,564	6,533	6,344	-20.7%
North Carolina	10,827	9,841	9,547	8,828	8,601	-20.6%
District of Columbia	2,197	2,217	2,111	2,066	1,797	-18.2%
Massachusetts	10,497	10,427	9,652	8,958	8,619	-17.9%
New York	30,072	29,493	27,992	26,783	24,962	-17.0%
Ohio	14,532	13,703	12,232	11,940	12,069	-16.9%

State	FY2007	FY2008	FY2009	FY2010	FY2011	% Change in Caseload FY2007-FY2011
Colorado	7,777	7,964	7,392	6,980	6,488	-16.6%
North Dakota	1,263	1,223	1,210	1,078	1,066	-15.6%
Louisiana	5,333	5,065	4,786	4,453	4,531	-15.0%
Connecticut	5,764	5,373	4,761	4,462	4,926	-14.5%
Washington	11,107	11,167	10,961	10,136	9,533	-14.2%
Alaska	2,126	1,954	1,851	1,765	1,829	-14.0%
Wisconsin	7,541	7,403	6,785	6,575	6,547	-13.2%
Nebraska	5,875	5,591	5,343	5,358	5,117	-12.9%
Kansas	6,631	6,306	5,691	5,979	5,852	-11.7%
South Dakota	1,566	1,482	1,484	1,485	1,407	-10.2%
Nevada	5,070	5,023	4,783	4,807	4,636	-8.6%
Kentucky	7,207	7,182	6,872	6,983	6,659	-7.6%
Oregon	9,562	8,988	8,650	9,001	8,871	-7.2%
Indiana	11,295	11,903	12,238	12,276	10,779	-4.6%
Utah	2,765	2,714	2,759	2,886	2,701	-2.3%
Tennessee	7,751	7,219	6,723	6,695	7,647	-1.3%
Illinois	17,864	17,843	17,080	17,730	17,641	-1.2%
Texas	30,137	28,154	26,686	28,947	30,109	-0.1%
West Virginia	4,432	4,412	4,237	4,112	4,475	1.0%
Arkansas	3,616	3,522	3,657	3,756	3,732	3.2%
Montana	1,737	1,600	1,639	1,723	1,794	3.3%
Missouri	10,282	7,607	8,667	9,880	10,620	3.3%
Mississippi	3,328	3,292	3,320	3,582	3,597	8.1%
Arizona	9,099	9,590	9,423	9,930	10,883	19.6%
TOTAL	488,285	463,799	421,350	406,412	400,540	-18.0%

Source: Table prepared by the Congressional Research Service based on caseload data by state, included in HHS, ACF, ACYF, Children's Bureau, "Foster Care FY2003-FY2011: Entries, Exits and Number of Children in Care on the Last Day of Each Fiscal Year by State" (data are as reported by states via AFCARS as of July 2012).

Table E-2. Children Waiting for Adoption, FY2007-FY2011, Percentage Change in the Number of Those Children and Share Adopted by State

States are ordered by change in number of waiting children (largest % decline to greatest % increase), FY2007-FY2011

State	Number of Children Waiting to be Adopted					% Change in Number of Waiting Children	Share of Children Waiting on Last Day of Previous Fiscal Year Who Were Adopted in	
	FY2007	FY2008	FY2009	FY2010	FY2011		FY2008	FY2011
Hawaii	733	555	428	351	277	-62.2%	49.2%	56.4%
Maryland	1,660	1,506	1,221	883	719	-56.7%	36.7%	60.0%
New Hampshire	325	297	272	227	167	-48.6%	51.4%	63.4%
Idaho	593	576	498	389	334	-43.7%	39.8%	66.6%
Minnesota	1,674	1,393	1,227	1,073	955	-43.0%	46.9%	54.1%
Illinois	5,598	4,608	2,728	2,944	3,272	-41.6%	26.3%	41.3%
Pennsylvania	3,408	3,525	2,943	2,551	2,045	-40.0%	61.3%	78.9%
California	20,830	17,847	15,664	14,872	12,881	-38.2%	37.3%	36.0%
Colorado	1,762	1,897	1,506	1,246	1,098	-37.7%	57.0%	75.0%
Florida	7,927	7,942	6,364	5,022	4,994	-37.0%	48.8%	58.6%
District of Columbia	560	493	486	419	357	-36.3%	20.2%	25.3%
Puerto Rico	1,145	1,071	956	903	746	-34.8%	13.3%	6.2%
Oregon	2,527	2,206	1,840	1,827	1,663	-34.2%	41.6%	36.0%
Rhode Island	400	415	333	310	267	-33.3%	65.0%	64.8%
Missouri	2,853	1,792	1,982	1,952	1,946	-31.8%	30.6%	61.4%
North Dakota	337	288	298	227	230	-31.8%	47.2%	52.4%
Michigan	6,115	5,674	4,902	5,236	4,237	-30.7%	44.7%	47.7%
New Jersey	3,262	3,009	2,694	2,464	2,294	-29.7%	38.8%	44.2%
Alabama	1,824	1,751	1,475	1,271	1,296	-28.9%	24.2%	34.6%
North Carolina	3,095	2,903	2,722	2,427	2,234	-27.8%	54.7%	60.3%
Georgia	2,162	2,244	1,802	1,690	1,567	-27.5%	62.0%	63.4%
Oklahoma	4,022	3,766	3,429	2,872	2,956	-26.5%	37.7%	45.1%
Ohio	3,762	3,477	3,380	3,013	2,789	-25.9%	43.5%	47.1%
Virginia	1,834	1,769	1,617	1,562	1,372	-25.2%	36.2%	48.3%
Vermont	257	225	231	180	196	-23.7%	70.8%	74.4%
Montana	597	521	537	495	460	-22.9%	40.5%	48.1%
Delaware	311	304	239	253	244	-21.5%	35.7%	37.5%
South Carolina	1,781	1,823	1,862	1,699	1,415	-20.6%	29.5%	34.6%
New Mexico	963	907	870	777	786	-18.4%	44.3%	45.2%

State	Number of Children Waiting to be Adopted					% Change in Number of Waiting Children	Share of Children Waiting on Last Day of Previous Fiscal Year Who Were Adopted in	
	FY2007	FY2008	FY2009	FY2010	FY2011		FY2008	FY2011
South Dakota	452	423	380	418	376	-16.8%	38.9%	40.2%
Maine	614	619	571	575	511	-16.8%	52.4%	51.5%
Iowa	1,299	1,158	1,003	1,068	1,088	-16.2%	80.1%	80.9%
New York	7,659	7,014	6,890	6,603	6,418	-16.2%	31.3%	33.5%
Wyoming	151	98	73	85	127	-15.9%	61.6%	85.9%
Kentucky	2,153	2,101	2,048	1,951	1,918	-10.9%	35.9%	42.2%
Indiana	3,210	3,090	3,224	3,192	2,886	-10.1%	46.8%	48.7%
Wisconsin	1,284	1,329	1,255	1,159	1,163	-9.4%	56.2%	61.9%
Massachusetts	2,868	2,846	2,839	2,758	2,672	-6.8%	24.8%	26.3%
Alaska	766	769	714	686	714	-6.8%	38.4%	42.9%
Mississippi	898	996	975	843	880	-2.0%	31.3%	42.5%
Washington	2,837	3,035	3,147	3,089	2,783	-1.9%	44.4%	51.2%
Utah	574	553	565	553	567	-1.2%	93.4%	104.3%
Texas	13,552	13,414	12,844	13,108	13,481	-0.5%	33.4%	36.0%
Kansas	1,812	1,960	1,852	1,825	1,817	0.3%	39.8%	42.8%
Nevada	1,936	2,200	2,098	2,094	1,968	1.7%	24.3%	39.2%
Louisiana	1,137	1,069	1,093	1,091	1,162	2.2%	52.4%	58.8%
Nebraska	805	881	831	768	831	3.2%	64.6%	53.8%
Arizona	2,516	2,323	2,792	2,673	2,822	12.2%	67.4%	85.1%
West Virginia	1,278	1,300	1,220	1,241	1,473	15.3%	40.9%	56.2%
Connecticut	1,162	1,430	1,354	1,245	1,341	15.4%	66.4%	49.1%
Tennessee	1,622	1,477	1,326	1,692	2,027	25.0%	64.5%	45.6%
Arkansas	780	872	850	1,604	1,414	81.3%	64.7%	36.8%
TOTAL	133,682	125,741	114,450	109,456	104,236	-22.0%	41.3%	46.2%

Source: Table prepared by the Congressional Research Service based on state-level data reported via AFCARS as of July 2012, included in HHS, ACF, ACYF, Children's Bureau, "Children in Public Foster Care Waiting to be Adopted" and "Adoptions of Children with Public Child Welfare Agency Involvement."

Notes: There is no definition in federal law or regulation for the term "waiting for adoption." For purposes of analysis, and as used in this table, the HHS, Children's Bureau counts as "waiting" any child in foster care with a case plan goal of adoption and/or to whom all parental rights have been terminated. However, it excludes from this count any youth 16 or older to whom all parental rights have been terminated if that youth has a case plan goal of "emancipation."

Although not true for every child, the very large majority of children adopted with public child welfare agency involvement were previously in foster care.

Author Contact Information

Emilie Stoltzfus
Specialist in Social Policy
estoltzfus@crs.loc.gov, 7-2324